Through Faith They Shall Overcome

An LDS Guide to Facing the Daunting Challenge of Forgiving Sexual Sin

Ruth Davidson

Gatehouse Media
367 W. 1450 N.
American Fork, Utah 84003

Through Faith They Shall Overcome

ISBN: 0-9743621-2-3

HISTORY
1st Edition: Summer 2005

PRINTED IN THE UNITED STATES OF AMERICA.
10 9 8 7 6 5 4 3 2 1   .

Graphic Design by
Jon Madsen
2812 N 600 E
Lehi, UT 84043
jmadsen@hotmail.com

*"Forgiveness is
the fragrance that the violet sheds
on the heel that has crushed it."*

—Mark Twain

Contents

NOTE

Names carrying an asterisk (*) are not real and are intended to maintain the anonymity of the person(s) involved in the examples and stories herein.

Through Faith They Shall Overcome

An LDS Guide to Facing the Daunting Challenge of Forgiving Sexual Sin

Ruth Davidson

1

"Upon My House Shall It Begin"
(D&C 112:25)

As the forces of evil have grown and spread across the face of the earth in these, the last days, countless children of God have fallen victim to the cunning plans of Satan which "he hath devised to ensnare the hearts of men" (Alma 28:13) in order to "lead them carefully down to hell." (2 Nephi 28:1) This is not only true of people of the world, but many members of The Church of Jesus Christ of Latter-day Saints have fallen victim to the destructive effects of Satan's clever schemes. This destruction is most evident in the prevalence of sexual sin and all of its devastating consequences. Pornography, masturbation, adultery, fornication, homosexuality, participation in prostitution, incest and molestation are only a few of the manifestations of this great scourge and have become increasingly rampant.

The Lord has powerfully declared, "Behold, I, the Lord, have looked upon you and have seen abominations in the church that profess my name." (D&C 50:4) One of His latter-day prophets, President Ezra Taft Benson, stated, "All is not well in Zion. As Moroni counseled, we must cleanse the inner vessel. . . The plaguing sin of this generation is sexual immorality. This, the

Prophet Joseph said, would be the source of more temptations, more buffetings, and more difficulties for the elders of Israel than any other. (See *Journal of Discourses, 8:55.*) President Joseph F. Smith said that sexual impurity would threaten the Church within—and so it does." (*Ensign*, May 1986, p. 4)

Countless and untold suffering has come about because of the growing prevalence of sexual immorality. These grievous iniquities not only affect those transgressors who have participated in them, but they affect each and every person surrounding those transgressors in profound and devastating ways. Broken marriages; emotional, physical or sexual abuse; divorce and abandonment are only some of the outward manifestations of the spiritual and emotional suffering that inevitably occurs when sexual sin is present. Turmoil, anguish, pain, depression, and other types of emotional, mental and spiritual suffering are fruits of these sins, as well. Many who have lived with transgressors have deep emotional scars and wounds arising from the grief and pain afflicted on them because of the unrighteous choices of others.

Despite all this, the Lord has given the divine directive to "forgive men their trespasses" so that "your heavenly Father will also forgive you." (Matthew 6:14) He tells us, "Ye ought to forgive one another; for he that forgiveth not his brother his trespasses standeth condemned before the Lord; for there remaineth in him the greater sin." (D&C 64:9) To one hurting, broken, devastated and betrayed by the sexual transgression of a spouse or other person, this admonition may seem beyond reach and impossible.

Truly, forgiveness often seems unobtainable in the aftermath of the cataclysmic emotions that arise after there has been any kind of betrayal or trauma brought about by sexual sin. It is essential to understand that when faced with the burdensome task of forgiving something of this nature, forgiveness, like striving for perfection, will be a process that takes much time, effort, energy, determination and power beyond one's own capacity to accomplish. Forgiveness will never be immediate and complete. Like anything that bears eternal fruit, forgiveness will come to the faithful "line upon line, precept upon precept" (D&C 98:12) through time, through a willing heart, and ultimately as a healing gift that will come through the power, grace and mercy of our Savior and Redeemer, the Lord Jesus Christ.

This book is intended to be a guide not only to those who are striving to heal families and relationships in the aftermath of sexual sin, but it is also meant to be a resource for those left alone and abandoned after there has been sexual sin present in a relationship. Though each path toward healing and forgiveness will be as varied and unique as every individual, there are guidelines and principles, that if understood, may help move one toward the healing that comes from forgiveness.

Knowledge and faith in our Savior is an essential part of this process because it is "because of thy faith in Christ, whom thou hast never before heard nor seen," that "thy faith (can make) thee whole." (Enos 1:7) We must trust that our Savior has the power and capacity to heal "the broken in heart, and (bind) up their wounds," (Psalm 147:3) that this is part of His eternal mission and plan. The Lord promises, "Unto you that fear my name shall the Sun of righteousness arise with healing in his wings." (Malachi 4:2) Those who have had to bear the consequences of the unrighteous choices of others can hold on to these sacred eternal promises with their whole souls, knowing that one day their hearts can be healed completely through the power and love of the healer of all wounds, the Savior Jesus Christ.

2

"Known Unto God Were All Their Cries, and All Their Sufferings" (Alma 60:10)

One woman expressed the following emotions several months after her husband had left her for another woman. She said, "I don't know why I continue to hurt so much after mine and (my husband's) separation. My husband has picked up and moved on with his life. Why can't I? I can barely do what I need to do to stay afloat and take care of my children. I continue to suffer great pain. I feel lost. Sometimes at night I'll have horrible, awful nightmares and when I wake up, I think, 'It's all real; it's not just a dream. This is real.'"

For those who have suffered similar wounds such as this woman's, it needs to be understood that the damage and destruction brought in by sexual sin are some of the deepest that could be inflicted on another's soul. There is a reason the Lord ranks sexual sin second only to murder. The consequences of these sins are some of the most horrific and damaging one can experience, whether that person is a transgressor or a victim of a transgressor's choices. Jeffrey R. Holland said:

> A(n). . .important scriptural observation is offered by the writer of Proverbs: "Can a man take fire in his bosom, and his clothes not be burned? Can one go

upon hot coals, and his feet not be burned? . . .Whoso committeth adultery. . .destroyeth his own soul. A wound and dishonor shall he get; and his reproach shall not be wiped away." (Proverbs 6:27-28; 32-33)

Why is the matter of sexual relationships so severe that fire is almost always the metaphor, with passion pictured vividly in flames? . . .We declare that one who uses the God-given body of another without divine sanction abuses the very soul of that individual, abuses the central purpose and processes of life. . . .In exploiting the body of another—which means exploiting his or her soul—one desecrates the Atonement of Christ. . . .And when one mocks the Son of Righteousness, one steps into a realm of heat hotter and holier than the noonday sun. (*Ensign,* Nov. 1998, p. 76)

The consequences of sexual sin are so catastrophic that when Alma spoke to his son, Corianton, regarding his sexual sins, he said, "Know ye not, my son, that these things are an abomination in the sight of the Lord; yea, most abominable above all sins save it be the shedding of innocent blood or denying the Holy Ghost?" (Alma 39:5) He later claims, "Whosoever *murdereth* against the light and knowledge of God, it is not easy for him to obtain a forgiveness." (Alma 39:6, italics added) Such strong language— murder—is used not only for describing what the transgressors' choices have done to their own souls but it can apply to the depth of severity of the harm they have done to other souls damaged spiritually by their choices.

Alma talks of the reality of this kind of spiritual "murder" during the time he was "racked with eternal torment" and "harrowed up to the greatest degree. . .with all [his] sins." He said pertaining to this time, "I did remember all my sins and iniquities, for which I was tormented with the pains of hell; yea, I saw that I had rebelled against my God, and that I had not kept his holy commandments. Yea, and I had *murdered* many of his children, or rather led them away unto destruction." (Alma 36:12-14, italics added)

Many are "led to destruction" because of the unrighteous choices of others, particularly in relation to sexual sin. The prophet Jacob in the *Book of Mormon*, while speaking to women whose husbands had been unfaithful to them, talks about this deep spiritual devastation. He stated, "Many hearts *died*, pierced with deep wounds." (Jacob 2:35, italics added) That statement so aptly describes the heartache and suffering that comes to those who are victims of these kinds of transgressions.

"Satan Hath Sought to Deceive You, That He Might Overthrow You" (D&C 50:3)

There are reasons why this kind of spiritual destruction happens to those persons surrounding a transgressor, whether or not they have participated in sin. In the *Doctrine & Covenants,* the Lord tells us, "Behold, verily I say unto you, there are hypocrites among you, who have deceived some, which has given the adversary power." (50:7) The adversary is truly given great power in transgressors' homes and lives because of the lies, deception and darkness that are repercussions of sexual sin. When transgressors sin in this way, those persons bring the presence of evil spirits into their homes because of their choices and actions. They are literally "surrounded by demons" and are "encircled about by the angels of him who hath sought to destroy. . .souls." (Helaman 13:38) These influences can affect all within the home or those who are bound to these transgressors by family ties, whether or not they are in the direct presence of the transgressor.

These evil spirits attack every person differently, but the results for each bear similar fruits. Fruits include oppression, darkness, turmoil, anguish, sorrow, sadness, discouragement, confusion, unrest, panic, anxiety, feelings of worthlessness, low self-esteem, anger, bitterness, contention, torment, misery, depression, despondency and so on. Elder David R. Snow compared these evil influences to "spiritual hurricanes" and said, "We place ourselves in the path of these spiritual hurricanes when we indulge in lust and licentiousness; promiscuity and pornography. . . .Then we are suddenly in the grip of their satanic power, and they lay waste our lives, bringing anguish and agony, depression, despair and desolation. Too many times they also bring sadness, sorrow, suffering and heartache to our loved ones." (*Ensign*, Nov. 1999, p. 31)

President David O. McKay, in a talk given at Brigham Young University on "Personal Radiation," described the way these types of dark influences come about through personal choices. He said:

> There is one responsibility which no man can evade; that responsibility is his personal influence. Man's unconscious influence is the silent, subtle radiation of personality—the effect of his words and his actions on others. This radiation is tremendous. Every moment of life man is changing, to a degree, the life of the whole world.
>
> Every man has an atmosphere which is affecting every other man. He cannot escape for one moment from this radiation of his character, this constant weakening or strengthening of others. Man cannot evade the responsibility by merely saying it is an unconscious influence.
>
> . . .This radiation, to which I refer, comes from what a person really is, not from what he pretends to be. Every man by his mere living is radiating either sympathy, sorrow, morbidness, cynicism, or happiness and hope or any one of a hundred other qualities.
>
> Life is a state of radiation and absorption. To exist is to radiate; to exist is to be the recipient of radiation. (April 27, 1948)

When dark influences are brought in by transgressors because of sin, those dark influences will affect each and every person in the home. Despite varied attacks, these dark influences will inevitably lead to torment and suffering if that person does not have the right tools to fight them. Some become desperate, despairing, discouraged, depressed and hopeless. Many become troubled, agitated or despondent; some become hostile, aggressive, angry and resentful. Other emotional problems or behavioral issues may arise, problems which may parade as social maladjustment, learning difficulties, feelings of insecurity or inadequacy, eating disorders and emotional or mental sicknesses. Many times intense preoccupation with superficial things—such as beauty, weight, popularity, prestige or wealth—to create feelings of worth will arise. Even the tendency toward the same sins or transgressions will often abound within the home environment, since the "author of all sin. . .doth carry on his works of darkness. . .from generation to generation, according as he can get hold upon the hearts of the children of men." (Helaman 7:22)

The attacks of Satan and his evil forces are diverse, but they all are designed for a specific purpose. Satan hopes to make all "miserable like unto himself" (2 Nephi 2:27) with the intent to "lead. . .souls to destruction." (D&C 10:22)

One woman spoke of the way she felt attacked by dark spirits brought into her home through feeling low self-worth and a deep lack of self-esteem for many, many years. "I always felt like I was less than everyone around me in almost all aspects of my life," she said. "I never felt pretty enough or thin enough or accomplished enough. In social situations, I felt inept and backward—like I would never fit in well or be socially graceful, no matter how hard I tried. As a mother, I would agonize over my lacks and what I didn't do for my children. I loved them with all my heart, but I felt I didn't have enough energy or strength to be the kind of mother they deserved or that I could serve them as I desired."

She continues, "Sometimes I would pray in desperation to Heavenly Father that He would help rid me of these feelings that seemed so oppressive and overwhelming. Sometimes they seemed to immobilize me and stop my progression. Once I found out about my husband's ongoing sexual sins, I finally realized that for many years I had fought against dark influences brought into our home because of his choices. This helped me realize the source behind what I was feeling. I could then better push the thoughts away, fighting them with all I had. In doing this, I've come to recognize that I am a valued daughter of God that He loves very much. He trusts me and is proud of the righteous efforts in my life, despite my weaknesses and shortcomings. I have felt great strength come to me in realizing that I have not been 'less' as a person because of what I've gone through. I've been in a dark battle and have gained great strength in overcoming the influences that have plagued our home."

Another woman spoke about a preoccupation regarding her physical appearance, particularly in relation to her weight, that became the way she felt continually attacked by darkness brought into her home by her husband's sinful choices. She became almost obsessed with feeling like she always needed to lose weight and that she never could. Often she felt like she could not even go out in public because of the way she looked and that she shouldn't go out until she got her life under control in this way. She even felt the intense impulse to turn to food to soothe or tranquilize the awful feelings regarding her weight was also related to the attacks she received.

Another woman spoke of always feeling less intellectually, that she'd never be smart enough to accomplish anything worthwhile or impacting. She often felt intimidated by others who seemed bright and articulate; she felt she could never add value in this way. She came to believe that others looked down on her and often judged her because of these lacks, as well. She felt stifled in social interactions because of these feelings and felt an overwhelming sense of inferiority.

As a further example, another woman who struggled with dark influences came to believe the past mistakes she'd made in her life could never be forgiven or taken away, that they would always make her less than others who'd tried to live righteously and that she'd always be judged and condemned for what she'd done. She felt plagued by reminders of how awful she must have been and still must be inside, that she could never be considered a pure daughter of God and have the blessings that came from living a righteous life.

In another instance one man, who struggled with similar influences, considered himself fat, lazy and unsuccessful. He felt his life was in a rut and that he could never break out of what he had turned out to be and gain the respect of those around him. He essentially felt worthless, unloved and of no importance.

These are just a few examples of what the influences of darkness and the adversary can do inside a home and in a heart. This destruction is real, often overwhelming, and sometimes overpowering. It must inevitably be fought first through the understanding of what is happening and then by the help and strength of the Lord and Savior, Jesus Christ, who promises to grant "power to overcome all things which are not ordained of him." (D&C 50:35) Until these dark influences are seen for what they are and the great destruction they can bring, they will continue to thwart and hurt those who become subjected to them.

"They Were Lifted Up in Pride, Even to the Persecution of Many of Their Brethren" (Helaman 3:33)

Another reason spiritual destruction occurs in relationships after sexual sin has been present is because transgressors often become tools of destruction to those around them. Their choices and actions have allowed them to lose the Spirit of the Lord in their lives. Elder H. Burke Peterson, in the October 1993 General Conference, described the process of losing the Spirit. Although he spoke of participation in pornography directly, the pattern he suggested may apply to any type of participation in sexual sin. He begins by saying that, after wrong choices have been made,

> . . .the light inside us grows dimmer because the darkness inside increases. The effect of this is that we cannot think as clearly on life's challenges—be they business, church, school, family, or personal—because the channel to the source of light for the solving of problems is cluttered. . . .Our entitlement to personal revelation on any subject is severely restricted. We don't do as well in school or at work. We are left more

on our own, and as a result we make more mistakes and we are not as happy. . . Hope and faith in Christ begin to fade, and more and more, turmoil and discontent become our companions.

Brothers, sisters, and parents are not as happy together as they used to be. We find less peace and contentedness in our hearts and homes. We do things that later we wish we had not done. Contention looms its vicious head, and when contention is present, the Spirit of Christ departs from us. (*Ensign,* Nov. 1993, p. 43)

When the Spirit of Christ departs, the adversary then has a chance to come in and take over. He then "whispereth in their ears, until he grasps them with his awful chains, from whence there is no deliverance." (2nd Nephi 28:22) Transgressors' thoughts and ideas quickly become tainted with the adversary's poison and venom. When this happens, transgressors inevitably turn on those around them and become tools of destruction to those within their reach.

Satan is clever and cunning in these attacks. He'll often convince transgressors that everyone outside themselves are the ones with the real problems and issues—never themselves directly. Transgressors are easily provoked to anger, bitterness, impatience and fault-finding in their interactions. Any blame for resulting contention, fighting or bickering will immediately be placed on the outside party, particularly a spouse in a marriage relationship. Outside parties will be attacked as emotionally or mentally unhealthy, as spiritually off base or socially inept, as unbalanced in their lives and behaviors, as incapable of true love and caring, as hypocritical, contentious, angry and spiteful. Sometimes they are criticized as ugly, overweight, an awful parent, shallow, superficial, or obsessive in spiritual or other matters. Outside parties will then be blamed by transgressors for their inability to work through the problems that have arisen because of these attacks. They are often accused of being blind to the problems they've created and that they lack the ability to see themselves as dysfunctional.

At this point, too, the adversary often convinces transgressors to use the negative behaviors and reactions evoked in others — anger or contention particularly, even if these were used solely as a defense — as the excuse needed for the transgressors' subsequent behaviors. This usually entails further sinful actions — in turning to another person outside the marriage relationship, for example, or perhaps engaging in pornography or other immoral behaviors. This may also be the transgressors' excuse to show that their marriages cannot be worked on and thus they need to leave them for their own well-being.

Transgressors' rationalization for these types of excuses usually fall into a pattern of thinking similar to this: "My marriage is awful. My spouse is so contentious, angry and vengeful. My spouse is blind to personal faults and shortcomings. It's destroying me, having to live with someone as awful as this. My spouse is dysfunctional and emotionally unstable. With all I've put up with, I shouldn't have to live like this. I deserve so much more. I deserve to be treated with love and appreciation. I am justified in anything I do to escape the kind of life my spouse has created for me." In essence, it is as if a transgressor is saying, "This is all your fault because of who you are and what you are — or what you aren't and what you never will be. You drove me to these kinds of choices — you, your lacks and your behaviors. You've given me many wounds; you don't fulfill my needs and you never will. I am entitled to something better, whatever that means."

Many marriages crumble because of these behaviors and actions; those marriages which don't are inevitably filled with contention, anger, manipulation, control, blame and the inability to truly work through issues and establish good working relationships. Even if a spouse is not blamed directly for sinful behavior by a transgressor, a spouse will still be condemned as unable to see his or her own faults and weaknesses that have created the problems in the relationship. Often problems or challenges from the past are rekindled, as well, even if solutions had previously been found.

Another way transgressors hurt those around them is, as the wicked Gadianton robbers tried to do to the Nephites, try to "cut them off from all their outward privileges" (3rd Nephi 4:16) and "put an end to (their) receiving. . .strength." (Alma 56:29) Often transgressors become more and more controlling of their spouses' activities, pulling them away from outside sources—such as friends, family or church members—that could bring strength to them. Transgressors often claim, "Our marriage is no one's business but our own," despite problems that may exist therein. They often refuse to become involved in family, social or church activities or may try to keep their spouses from becoming involved. In essence, transgressors often try to control their spouses' activities, behaviors and outside relationships, attempting to make them fit into parameters of their own choosing. They purposefully isolate them from needed outside strength.

Another subtle means of destruction occurs when transgressors get so caught up in their sins and addictive patterns that those things become the central focus of their lives, blocking out all righteousness. They show no concern, caring or true love for their spouses or family members. Though they might not engage in direct negative attacks, they become withdrawn and secretive, living an isolated life—consumed in their sins and selfishness. In this process, they are sending the silent message that, "You are not valued to me. I do not care for you, nor do you have meaning in my life. You are not the focus of my time and attention. I have other things that are more important to me." These behaviors, too, are as damaging and hurtful as other direct attacks and destroy the foundation upon which strong relationships must be built.

There are multitudes of ways and means to hurt or harm, but transgressors will become tools of destruction to those around them when they are open to the adversary's influence. President Gordon B. Hinckley, while a First Counselor in the First Presidency, spoke of the kind of destruction that occurs in a marriage relationship when a partner has been unfaithful through adultery or other sins. He spoke of the time he worked for a "full decade" in the "task of sitting in judgment on the worthiness of those who come back into the Church after having been excommunicated." He described a specific relationship in which a wife and a husband, both active members of the church, had married in the temple and had five beautiful children. After eighteen years of marriage, a marriage described as "sometimes sweet and sometimes difficult," the husband chose to leave his wife and family. President Hinckley quoted the wife's experience, as reported in a letter to him. She said:

> (My husband) decided that he never loved me and that our marriage was a mistake from the beginning. He was convinced that there was nothing in our relationship for him. He filed for divorce and moved out. "Wait," I kept saying. "Oh, no. Stop! Don't do this. Why are you leaving? What is wrong? Please, talk to me. Look at our children. What of all our dreams? Remember our covenants. No, no! Divorce is not the answer." He would not hear me. I thought I would die.
>
> Now I am a single parent. What an enormous load of heartache, pain, and loneliness are behind that statement. It explains so much trauma and so much anger from my teenage sons. It explains so many tears from my little girls. It explains so many sleepless nights, so many family demands and needs. Why am I in this mess? What did I do wrong? How will I ever get through school? How will I get through this week? Where is my husband? Where is the father of my children? I join the ranks of tired women whose husbands leave them. I have no money, no job. I have children to care for, bills to pay, and not much hope.

President Hinckley later states regarding these kinds of devastating wounds:

> Some men. . .throw to the wind the most sacred and solemn of covenants, entered into in the house of the Lord and sealed under the authority of the holy priesthood. They set aside their wives who have been faithful, who have loved and cared for them, who have struggled with them in times of poverty, only to be

discarded in times of affluence.

. . .Do I sound harsh and negative? Yes, I feel that way, as I deal with case after case and have done so over a period of time. . . .Now I recognize that there may be some few cases where conditions of the marriage are totally intolerable. But these cases are in the minority. . . .The complaint of a husband, after eighteen years of marriage and five children, that he no longer loves his wife is, in my judgment, a feeble excuse for the violation of covenants made before God and also the evasion of the responsibilities that are the very strength of the society of which we are a part. The finding of fault with consequent divorce is usually preceded by a long period in which little mistakes are spoken of in harsh and angry language, where tiny molehills of difference grow into great mountains of conflict. I am satisfied that the more unkindly a wife is treated, the less attractive she becomes. She loses pride in herself. She develops a feeling of worthlessness. Of course it shows. (*Ensign,* Nov. 1991, pp. 50-51)

These are the kinds of tragedies that occur when transgressors have been unfaithful and have participated in sexual sin. They become tools of destruction "to be carried about by the temptations of the devil whithersoever he desire(s) to carry them, and to do whatsoever iniquity he desire(s) they should." (3rd Nephi 6:17) As this kind of tool, they not only damage themselves further but they hurt those they live with—or those they've left behind because of their choices.

"And as the Covenant Which They Made Unto Me Has Been Broken, Even so it Has Become Void and of None Effect" (D&C 54:4)

There is a third reason transgressors' choices of sexual sin lead to great and devastating destruction. When sacred marital covenants are violated this deeply, it literally destroys a marriage and the foundation of love, commitment and trust that must be part of a healthy, viable relationship. This destruction is dark, grievous and long-lasting, affecting not only the partners in the marriage but the children, families, extended families and friends about them. Rebuilding after this kind of destruction, if such is possible, is a process that will take months and years, not days and weeks.

No one in this world can share anything more sacred or personal than physical intimacy with another human being. It is this gift of physical intimacy, coupled with emotional and spiritual righteousness and oneness, that can ultimately lead a couple toward the highest state of happiness and completeness that the Lord can bestow on any of his children. Elder Jeffrey R. Holland described intimacy as "the ultimate symbol of total union, a totality and a union ordained and defined by God. From the Garden of Eden onward, marriage was intended to mean the complete merger of a man and a woman—their hearts, hopes, lives, love, family, future, everything. . . .This is a union of such completeness that we use the word *seal* to convey its eternal promise." (*Ensign*, Nov. 1998, p. 76)

When someone desecrates this type of physical intimacy through sexual sin, the use of pornography or other sexual perversions, that person is violating the most precious gift another person could give to them under the covenant of marriage. This great loss brings severe heartache to the victims wounded and betrayed by those with whom they have made sacred covenants. For a victim, it is as if he or she gave everything that could be possibly given physically, emotionally and spiritually, and that precious gift was betrayed, mocked and treated as something of no value.

The devastation from this loss is real and far-reaching. It can produce feelings and emotions similar to experiencing a loved one's death, a death which requires a lengthy process of grieving, healing and recovery. It can also make someone question innately his or her worth as a person. When a person is rejected and betrayed on such an intimate, personal level, it can produce inward questions such as, "Am I valued? Am I truly of worth? If someone could betray me on this level, does it mean I am not good enough, that my offerings as a person are not sufficient?" Great and searing wounds occur in those who have been betrayed like this, and deep and intense suffering does, as well.

It is little wonder that Satan would take the highest gift that could be given by another and destroy that gift by polluting it through sexual sin. He knows the devastation and wounds it produces; he knows the pain and suffering left in its wake. He knows the depression, feelings of inadequacy or worthlessness, and the desperation sexual sin can produce in victims. He also knows the darkness that can be perpetuated through transgressors who have bought into Satan's lies and deceptions, darkness that destroys not only their own souls but often the souls of those around them.

Satan knows the power and entrapment of sexual sin and how it can be that "flaxen cord" he places about a neck to lead someone toward greater and greater sin, sin that will soon become Satan's "strong cords" that will bind transgressors forever (2 Nephi 26:22) if they do not repent. Truly, sexual sin has destroyed not only individual families and individual lives, but it has destroyed nations and civilizations. As Neal A. Maxwell once stated:

> . . .Historian John Lukacs perceptively warned that sexual immorality was not merely a marginal development, but instead, was at the center of the moral crisis of our time (*The Passing of the Modern Age,* p. 169*)* Some thought Lukacs was overstating it, but consider the subsequent and sobering tragedy of children having children, of unwed mothers, of children without parents, of hundreds of thousands of fatherless children, and of rampant spousal infidelity. These and related consequences threaten to abort society's future even before the future arrives. (*Ensign,* May 1995, p. 69)

Therefore, "Turn, all ye Gentiles, from your wicked ways; and repent of your evil doings, of your lyings and deceivings, and of your whoredoms, and of your secret abominations. . .and come unto me, . . .that ye may receive a remission of your sins, and be filled with the Holy Ghost, that ye may be numbered with my people who are of the house of Israel." (3 Nephi 30:2)

3

"Ye Have Broken the Hearts of Your Tender Wives" (Jacob 2:35)

Janae and Doug* (*names have been changed) dated while they were in high school and wrote to each other during Doug's mission. Several months after Doug's return, the two of them married in the temple and started a family. They had the normal up's and down's of married life, balancing Tom's career and Janae's duties as a stay-at-home mother. They stayed active and involved in the church, finding joy and satisfaction in their mutual devotion to the gospel.

After they'd had several children and the oldest child hit the late teen years, one of the women Doug had dated in high school happened to move into their ward with her husband and young family. This woman's family, too, was active and involved in the church. This woman ended up serving in various positions in the ward and then became the Relief Society President.

During a church social function in which all the families of the ward were involved, something occurred which would soon result in the break-up of these two families. Doug and the woman he had dated in high school "happened to look at each other across the way and still realized there were feelings between the two of them."

Unbeknownst to anyone but themselves, they began a

relationship that quickly became adulterous. As a result, both of their marriages were destroyed and they left activity in the church. Doug and this woman never moved toward a marriage themselves, but they never got back with their respective partners.

Janae found herself alone, penniless, and suddenly carrying the full responsibility of being the sole provider for her large family. Doug became bitter, angry and contentious toward her, blaming her for all of the troubles and trials in his life and their marriage. He basically abandoned her and his children, rarely seeing them and not participating in any of their activities. Janae felt great pain and confusion over the breakup of her family and felt bewildered over how quickly it had happened.

Now, many years later, Janae still feels like she struggles with the wounds, hardship and devastation her husband left behind because of his choices. Her children still feel the absence of their father and have never seen any renewed commitment from him to become a part of their lives.

* * *

Kelsey grew up in a family where her father began having an affair shortly after his marriage to her mother. Though members of the church, Kelsey's family always stayed more on the fringes and never actively participated in it. For years as Kelsey grew up, her parent's marriage was marked by contention, anger, bitterness and abusive behaviors. Her father's interactions with her and her siblings remained harsh and volatile.

Kelsey ended up marrying a man who was not a member of the church. Her marriage did not last long, however, because her new husband had an affair on her. Reeling in pain because of this, she found herself married again but felt "empty and unfulfilled" with many internal wounds. Shortly afterward, she found herself doing what her father and first husband had done; she had an affair on her new husband. That marriage, too, ended in divorce.

After feeling genuine remorse over her decisions, Kelsey did all she could to become a member of the church in good standing. She sought the Lord in her own life and vowed to become closer to Him. Not long after this, she met another man who'd had a troubled past. His addiction to pornography as a young man had led him to subsequent promiscuity, but he wanted to clean up his life and become strong and active. Together they decided to marry in the temple and begin an eternal family, one based on the principles of the gospel. They both wanted to rebuild anew after their troubled pasts and start fresh and clean.

Several years and two children into her last marriage, Kelsey felt confused as to why her life seemed to be filled with so much contention and heartache. She and her husband fought often, they rarely shared intimacy or emotional closeness, and her husband seemed genuinely unhappy with her. He criticized and put her down almost constantly, many times leaving the home in anger and frustration. Not long after this, Kelsey discovered that her husband had fallen back into his addiction to pornography and had become heavily involved in it.

Not wanting to break up their eternal family—and knowing personally the struggle of overcoming sexual sin, Kelsey committed to her husband and the Lord that she would "help (her husband) get through his problems, no matter what." For awhile, her husband found great strength in her commitment to help him. He became open and honest with her about his struggles, seeking her out often for her support and strength. His addiction had become so strong and deep that conquering it became a daily battle they fought together. Sometimes Kelsey would have to sit with him as he "curled up in a ball on the floor, rocking back and forth" as he struggled to overcome the intense grip of his dependency. With Kelsey's help, her husband seemed to develop a determination for spirituality and cleanliness.

This determination didn't last beyond a few months, however. Kelsey noticed an abrupt change in his behavior as he suddenly became secretive and contentious toward her once again, turning against her in bitterness and anger—especially when she questioned him or attempted to continue to help him. Though he never admitted it openly—and in fact lied blatantly about it, Kelsey knew her husband had fallen back into his addiction once more.

Despite Kelsey's unwavering intentions to continue to work on their marriage—and her genuine love and caring for her husband, he decided he needed to separate from her. He told her "he never felt peace in her presence," that she always made life miserable for him and that she had left him—like everyone else in her past—worse off for having known her.

After a few months of separation, Kelsey's husband came to her and told her that the "only way he could ever become happy" was by "leaving her" because of the awful person she had become. Using this reasoning as his excuse, he filed for divorce. A few days after their divorce was final, he began dating other women. Scarcely a few weeks beyond that, he began an affair with another woman who had recently left her own husband.

Kelsey's ex-husband now blames Kelsey for the breakup of their marriage. He accuses her of ruining his life, saying she's left a "string" of destruction in her wake because of how selfish, dysfunctional, and horrible she's always been. In almost every interaction they have, Kelsey is blamed and attacked by her husband, who refuses to compromise with her on financial or childcare issues. He speaks openly of his disgust for her and has tried to turn his own family and mutual friends against her.

* * *

Megan had always considered herself as someone committed completely to her husband, Ryan, and her children. She had been a stay-at-home mother and had found contentment from her choice to do this. Though she and Ryan had struggled in their marriage occasionally throughout the years, they were issues she felt they had always been able to overcome. Although Megan admitted she had felt some lack of fulfillment in their relationship, she had always attributed it to Ryan's excessive time spent away from her and the family in meeting the demands of his work and career.

Despite these lacks, Megan still felt overall that she and Ryan had a good partnership. They were both active members of the church and had raised their children to become active members, as well. Both Megan and Ryan had held responsible positions of leadership and had labored together in fulfilling them.

After many years of marriage, however, Megan suddenly discovered that her husband, Ryan, had led a secret life throughout their whole marriage, a life filled with deception and dishonesty. He'd become addicted to pornography early on, and that addiction had led him to more serious sin in places and situations that further compromised their covenants and marriage.

Megan suddenly felt as if all of her foundations had been shattered, as if she had been building on something that had never existed. The hurt and pain she experienced from this betrayal was exquisite. Not only did she feel she had lost trust in someone she had loved deeply, she suddenly found that their relationship had never been what she assumed it had been. There were now serious, deep and explosive issues between the two of them, and she quickly discovered they did not have the capacity to resolve them.

Though both Megan and Ryan chose to stay and work on their relationship, this decision became a daily struggle that included contention, anger, blame, misunderstanding, distrust, tears, further hurt and deeper wounds. Megan felt Ryan didn't understand the pain and suffering she was going through because of his choices or that he didn't see the seriousness of what he'd done; Ryan didn't feel Megan understood him or acknowledged his attempts to cleanse his life and become closer to the Savior. He also felt she did not see or appreciate his genuine efforts to try and heal their marriage and family and that she would always "hold his sins over his head."

Megan and Ryan continue to work on their relationship and healing their marriage, but they find they often reach impasses while trying to work with each other. They acknowledge a mutual lack of trust and the inability to communicate and understand each other effectively. They don't want to give up their marriage, but they often feel helpless and hopeless in knowing how to move forward.

* * *

Heidi had married her husband in the temple and loved him with all of her heart. She was committed to him and their three sons with everything she had to give, serving them daily as a mother and a wife. As she looks back on her life, she doesn't even know how to explain the changes that happened in her marriage. All she knows is that her husband began finding fault with her and criticizing her in everything she did—from motherhood to the way she dressed. He constantly chastised her for her lacks and what she didn't give him to help him stay happy. He became emotionally and verbally abusive toward her, putting her down for who she was and what she had become. In tandem with this, he began losing his faith and testimony and became less and less involved in the church—ultimately denouncing his membership.

As Heidi struggled to deal with all the contention in her marriage and home—and the other unwise choices of her husband, she became increasingly confused and distressed. As a consequence, she lost a great deal of weight that put her physical health in jeopardy. She subsequently developed an eating disorder.

Her husband soon after abandoned her and filed for divorce, turning his own extended family against her "because of all of her lies" and the "terrible person and mother" she was. He berated her for her lack of control over her life, particularly in relation to her eating disorder, saying it showed what a dysfunctional person she had become. He wasn't about to "sit around and watch her destroy herself" and be subjected to her emotionally.

Heidi's husband never told her that he had been involved in any type of sexual immorality, but his relationship with another woman—who also planned on divorcing her own husband—soon came to the fore as they began seeing each other and living together outside the bonds of marriage. He told Heidi directly once, after he had left her and they had to work through divorce and custodial issues, "Anything that hurts you makes me happy." He withheld money, possessions and even some of her personal belongings from her. He also vowed to "replace her in his life as soon as possible," claiming he hoped to erase all evidence and memories of her.

Heidi currently struggles with the deep, internal wounds

she's received as she tries to rebuild her life and take care of her three young sons. She is left to provide for them and their needs while grappling with intense, consuming injuries of her own. She often sheds tears over how inadequate and worthless she feels as a person and she wonders how—or if—she'll ever be happy again. She also wonders if another marriage and relationship would end in the same way, and does not know if she would want to risk opening up herself in such a way again.

* * *

Jill had many years invested in her husband and temple marriage when she found out her husband had participated in an affair for a few years of their married life. He only stopped his affair when it was discovered. Jill felt devastated at his betrayal and suffered tremendous heartache and pain. For some time, she wavered between leaving their tempestuous relationship or staying with her husband. After much grief, struggle and anguish, both she and her husband decided to stay together and rebuild their marriage for the sake of their children.

Jill's husband went through an excommunication process and was then re-baptized, making many positive changes in his life throughout this process. Though Jill and her husband are still together, her husband will often blame her for petty problems and differences in their marriage and occasionally belittles her in front of others. Despite these minor injuries, Jill feels she loves her husband deeply. She is genuinely content with their marriage and she never plans on leaving. She feels that she and her husband have overcome his past mistakes and believes they no longer play a part in their lives.

* * *

Debbie's husband had an affair on her after they'd been married in the temple and had five beautiful children together. Heartbroken and devastated, Debbie wondered how to rebuild her life and marriage but committed to try, leaning more fully on her testimony of the Savior and her commitment to the gospel. After attempts to heal their broken relationship, however, Debbie's husband participated in a second affair, claiming it was Debbie's fault because "she could never forgive me after my first affair and open her heart to me again. I could never work with her." Debbie was then abandoned by him and left as a single mother to raise her children on her own.

* * *

Each of the foregoing true accounts shows varied experiences of couples whose lives have been damaged by sexual sin. Whatever the experience has been, each person wounded or victimized in these incidents is under the same strong admonition of the Savior—to "forgive, if ye have ought against any: that your Father also which is in heaven may forgive you your trespasses." (Mark 11:25)

Most understand that forgiveness is necessary for one's own personal salvation, but for those grieving and grappling with these kinds of losses, abuses and betrayals, sometimes forgiveness seems unreachable—almost unobtainable. How does someone forgive another's sexual sin when that person not only leaves a marriage but continues to spew bitter hatred and venom, blaming a spouse for the darkness and upheaval that has come into their lives and marriage? How does one forgive harsh attacks that come daily—sometimes hourly, attacks designed to hurt, oppress, wound or torment? How does someone forgive a person "who has set at naught the counsels of God, and has broken the most sacred promises which were made before God" (D&C 3:13) by desecrating a covenant marriage through leaving it or betraying it? Even if a transgressor desires to repent and become clean again, how does someone forgive someone who has participated in sexual sin that is "second only to the shedding of blood in the category of personal crimes?" (*Gospel Doctrine,* 5th ed., p. 310)

Forgiveness, as stated before, is an ongoing, complicated process that will never be immediate and complete at the onset. In fact, like the command to become perfect "even as your Father which is in heaven is perfect," (Matthew 5:48) forgiveness is a process that may last beyond this life and extend into eternity. Even if forgiveness does not take that long to complete, coming to a full forgiveness will always require a great deal of time, effort, resolve, a willing and contrite heart, and most importantly the strength, help and insights from a loving Savior who will lead someone step by step—sometimes inch by inch—toward the healing that comes from this necessary step.

Forgiveness has been defined as "to pardon, or cease to feel resentment against; to. . .overlook a debt or trespass; to be merciful." (*Webster's New Dictionary*, p. 224) This "pardoning" and "overlooking a debt or trespass" for serious and grievous sexual sins can only begin with a deep and abiding trust in our Savior's atonement, for He is the One anointed by our Father in Heaven not only to "make reconciliation for the sins of the people" (Hebrews 2:18) but "to heal the broken-hearted,. . .to set at liberty them that are bruised." (Luke 4:18) There must exist a firm belief that the Savior truly does have the power and capacity to heal hearts which have been wounded this deeply, particularly those hearts that have carried the grief and pain of wounds inflicted on them by the unrighteous choices of others. Elder Richard G. Scott has promised, "The atonement will not only help us overcome our transgressions and mistakes, but in His time, it will resolve all inequities of life—those things that are unfair which are the consequences of circumstance or others' acts and not our own decisions." (*Ensign,* May 1997, p. 53) It is only with this knowledge—that the Savior will heal wounds, that He will resolve every inequity and injustice that has befallen His children because of the sinful choices of others—that will help those wounded move forward toward even the desire to forgive sexual sin.

James E. Faust has said:

> The atonement not only benefits the sinner but also benefits those sinned against—that is, the victims. By forgiving those who trespass against us, the atonement brings a measure of peace and comfort to those who have been innocently victimized by the sins of others.

> Some injuries are so hurtful and deep that they cannot be healed without help from a higher power and

hope for perfect justice and restitution in the next life.
(*Ensign,* Nov. 2001, p. 18, italics added)

The Savior does not ask His sons and daughters to forgive with the expectation that the trauma, wounds, betrayals and hurts should be immediately forgotten and dismissed; instead, He asks for the perfect trust to believe that when things are given to Him, He will resolve each and every issue with perfect judgment and equity. He wants us to believe in His ordained power to right every wrong, to heal every wounded heart and to restore every loss that has been experienced. Forgiveness can be borne by this belief—that He can and will do this for all those who are faithful unto His name.

Aubrey had an experience which helped her understand this concept—that the Lord would resolve every injury and all the unjust persecution that had come to her from her husband after he left her because of deep sexual sin. Several months after their divorce, while Aubrey's ex-husband lived in an adulterous relationship with another woman, he and Aubrey had to work through a childcare issue that came up. He wanted to change the conditions of a previous childcare arrangement, but Aubrey felt she could not compromise in the matter or it would end up hurting her. After her repeated refusals to give in to his demands, her ex-husband became bitterly angry toward her. He swore at her repeatedly and continued a demeaning tirade in which he accused her of being spiteful, self-righteous and contentious. He further blamed her for being a neglectful, lazy mother who only thought of herself and never her children or their needs. He then claimed it was because of those reasons—and because of the awful person and wife she'd been—that he'd had to leave the marriage. He told her that he could have never been happy with her. He then ended the call by hanging up angrily on her.

After the conversation, Aubrey felt emotionally crushed. She couldn't help but weep. Her heart felt shattered and broken. To still see the bitter hatred, resentment, anger and animosity her husband harbored for her—even after sincere efforts to work amicably with him—was devastating. She still felt she loved him and she grieved over the loss of their previous relationship. All he did was blame, criticize and loathe her, and no matter what she did, his opinion of her didn't change. She doubted it ever would.

In order to deal with the vulnerable emotions she felt, Aubrey asked for a priesthood blessing to help her through this difficult time. The blessing gave her great strength and promises that became a spiritual anchor for her. The Lord, first off, told her that He did not take the pain and suffering of one of His daughters lightly, that "each tear was a prayer unto Him" and that He would answer those prayers. The Lord told her that He, too, had been accused of "having a devil" by those He had come to love and save. He then reminded her that those who had judged Him would one day know of His power and acknowledge Him as the Savior.

The Lord then promised Aubrey that everything said wrongfully against her "would one day be accounted for, through either repentance or chastisement." He told her that in His eyes, she was pure before Him and that it was His opinion—and no one else's—that truly mattered. He then reminded her of His tender love for her and that she was a valued, treasured gem, one He would carefully guard and watch over. He assured her that He would always be with her to walk with her through the circumstances of her life—no matter what.

Aubrey came to learn from this that she could turn all of her injuries and hurts over to the Savior, knowing He would take care of each and every one and that He would one day handle them with perfect equity and justice. When she knew she could trust Him to do this for her, she could then let the burden of her sufferings go to Him. She came to experience, as others have, that "as ye are partakers of the sufferings, so *shall ye be also* of the consolation." (2nd Corinthians 1:7) "For as the sufferings of Christ abound in us, so our consolation also aboundeth by Christ." (2nd Corinthians 1:5)

"Judgment is Mine. . .and Vengeance is Mine, and I Will Repay" (Mormon 8:20)

Another important aspect of moving toward forgiveness is understanding that judgment and retribution for sexual transgression belongs solely to our Lord and Savior, Jesus Christ, for He is the only one authorized to be the perfect judge of our souls. Pertaining to those wounded by sexual sin, this means, as Dallin H. Oaks stated, that "mortals must refrain from judging any human being in the final sense of concluding or proclaiming that he or she is irretrievably bound for hell or has lost all hope of exaltation. . . .The gospel is a gospel of hope, and none of us is authorized to deny the power of the Atonement to bring about a cleansing of individual sins, forgiveness, and a reformation of life on appropriate conditions." (*BYU Devotional,* March 1998)

Not casting judgment also means realizing that as mortal individuals, our judgment of others will never be perfect and complete. Correct judgment becomes impossible with our limited understanding, knowledge and perceptions. We can never fully know the backgrounds, past circumstances, injuries or other factors that may have led someone to make the wrong choices he or she did. For example, one woman felt great frustration and anger for a man who left his marriage of over twenty years for a younger woman. She felt critical of his harshness, arrogance and pride. Whenever she heard about the hurt he still caused his family by his continued sins and his lack of remorse for them, she grew more and more disgusted with him. It wasn't until some years later that she learned that this man had been abused as a young man of twelve and that he carried many internal wounds from this. Knowing even these limited details, she came to understand more fully that she could never accurately judge someone or their subsequent choices without the Savior's insights, love and compassion to guide her.

It should be noted that withholding judgment of transgressors never means that someone can't stand firmly against evil and its destructive consequences. However, standing boldly and fighting against evil does not include attacking the soul of a transgressor in hatred, retaliation or revenge. A transgressor, too, is a beloved child of God whom He desires to save and one He will never abandon.

What Forgiveness Is; What Forgiveness Is Not

Forgiveness could ultimately be defined, then, as the process of learning to completely leave transgressors, their choices, their sins and the wrongs inflicted by them in the capable hands of the Savior, trusting that He will take "all things" and allow them to "work together for good" (D&C 100:15) to those who trust in Him. It is also the belief that the Savior will one day solve all the earthly afflictions, pains and sorrows caused by those transgressors with perfect justice and equity. Forgiveness moves from that level toward an active hope that one day transgressors will become healed and whole through the mercy and grace of the atoning blood of the Savior, Jesus Christ; it is the desire that those transgressors' lives will be cleansed of sin and darkness and become pleasing unto the Lord. Ultimately, forgiveness entails learning to love transgressors with "charity," the "pure love of Christ" which "endureth forever" and which brings those who "are possessed of it" (Moroni 7:46, 47) closer unto the Savior—the "fountain of all righteousness" (Ether 12:28) Unfeigned love, selflessness, patience, compassion, understanding, peace and hope are fruits of this kind of charity.

It must be remembered that forgiveness is a long, continual process of learning and growing toward the Savior and His light; it is not an immediate destination that occurs at the onset just for the asking. It may take a lifetime—or possibly into eternity—to master.

Just as it's important to understand what forgiveness is, it's also imperative to understand what forgiveness is *not*. Forgiveness does not necessarily entail the healing of a relationship, family or marriage—although forgiveness is an essential step toward that end. Yet a woman whose husband leaves her abused, alone and abandoned is under the same obligation to forgive as the woman whose husband tries to cleanse his life, repent and rebuild a marriage. Each one respectively can learn to adopt an active hope that those transgressors who betrayed them will be healed by the Savior, but that does not necessarily mean their own relationships are cleansed and will become whole again. In other words, forgiveness cannot be equated with where a relationship is at in terms of healing.

It is also necessary to understand that forgiveness does not mean blindly living with or putting up with continuing transgression, criticism, emotional or physical abuse, anger, blame, manipulation or control. The Lord never expects His children to subject themselves to the continued unrighteousness of others but vows to "lead away the righteous out from among (them)" (Jacob 2:3) if transgressors do not repent. In other words, forgiveness is not turning a blind eye and pretending abuses or offenses do not exist. Those abuses and offenses must ultimately be forgiven, but it does not mean that one must remain subjected to them.

Another important element to understand is that forgiveness does not mean that trust is automatically renewed or rekindled in a relationship where such trust has been violated. Forgiveness becomes the precursor to the willingness to work to rebuild that trust, but trust does not magically return with the demand of a transgressor for someone to "forgive." Trust must be rebuilt and re-earned over a lengthy period of time and become the byproduct of consistent righteous action.

Finally, forgiveness does not mean dismissing the problems that have arisen in relationships where there have been wounds, injuries, hurt and suffering caused by betrayals; those deep issues must be worked through item by item and resolved. Problems should never be thrown out under the guise that those sinned against need to "forgive and forget" in order to move forward. In essence, forgiveness is not ignoring feelings, hurts, damages and injuries by bypassing them as something that should not exist if forgiveness is present.

In summary, then, forgiveness is a lengthy, ongoing process in which someone learns to turn a transgressor and the wounds inflicted by that transgressor over to the Savior for all judgment and restitution; forgiveness then moves a person toward an active hope for a transgressor's spiritual well-being and ultimately charity for that person. On the other hand, forgiveness cannot be equated with where a relationship is at in terms of its healing, nor does it mean ignoring the issues or feelings that betrayals have caused. Forgiveness does not bring automatic trust or entail blindly living with continued transgression or with a transgressor who is unwilling to change abusive, controlling behaviors.

Forgiveness is a process that the Savior promises to help His children through, for "he giveth no commandments unto the children of men, save he shall prepare a way for them that they may accomplish the thing which he commandeth them." (1st Nephi 3:7) He truly will help each and every child in his or her individual quest to forgive and promises that "they shall overcome all things" (D&C 76:60) with His help and strength. One woman, whose husband had left her because of his adulterous relationship with another woman, was reassured of being able to reach this height in a blessing that foretold that "one day she would have an active desire for the welfare and salvation of her previous husband." This helped her through the process of learning to forgive when she realized there would come the day when her heart had healed enough from her pain and suffering to be able to accomplish this. This promise can be available to all through the redeeming power of our Savior's atonement. As Neal A. Maxwell once stated, "Jesus fully understands! His empathy is perfect! He knows how to help us!" (*Ensign,* Oct. 2001, p. 14)

4

"Cursed is He That Putteth His Trust in Man, or Maketh Flesh His Arm" (2ⁿᵈ Nephi 28:31)

There is a unique challenge to forgiving sexual sin that will come to any who try to rebuild a relationship after there has been sexual sin present therein. Those victimized or betrayed in relationships must realize they can never judge where they are at in the forgiveness process through the eyes, judgments and opinions of transgressors—or those people whose thinking transgressors have been able to sway. It is only through the Savior that they can have an accurate view of themselves and where they are at or need to be. If they do not gain the assurance they need from the Savior—and the Savior alone—that they stand approved of in His sight, they will never have the inward fortitude they need to begin to forgive and thus move toward healing a relationship.

This occurs for a very specific reason. Whenever sexual sin has been present in a relationship, the transgressor has compromised—and has many times lost—the ability to feel the influence of the Spirit of the Lord in his or her life. That means, in essence, that Satan has been allowed to blind and deceive, leading transgressors to specific patterns of thinking that are not in alignment with the will of the Lord. A transgressor's judgment and reasoning have become skewed by Satan's whisperings, his darkness and his lies. A transgressor then judges his interactions and the circumstances around him through this darkness and tainted thinking, which will never be accurate until the light of Christ comes back completely and fully into that transgressor's life. This will never happen immediately and takes a long to accomplish as a transgressor willingly and humbly tries to overcome the darkness in his soul.

Until Christ's light comes in and heals transgressors' ways of thinking, then, their judgments will always be distorted and inaccurate. For example, Satan often leads transgressors to blame their choices and difficulties they find themselves in on events and people outside themselves. Even if they do take responsibility for their wrong choices, they have usually minimized the consequences, the depth of severity and the damage of those choices, allowing Satan to tell them "this is not that big of deal. You didn't really cross the line. If you did cross the line, don't worry. You can easily repent."

Often the adversary convinces transgressors that their spouses have created the lacks in their relationships that have caused them to need to look outside those relationships to meet their needs. They may claim their spouses are spiritually off base, emotionally unstable, dysfunctional, unable to show true love and affection, or full of contention, anger and bitterness. Sometimes transgressors claim that their spouses have never appreciated all of the efforts they've made in their lives and that their spouses have never loved and valued them as they're supposed to be loved and valued in marriage. Often transgressors claim they must leave their current spouses or they will be destroyed by them. These and other excuses often become part of transgressors' thoughts and patterns of thinking.

The following are some examples of this distorted, inaccurate thinking. In one instance, a woman who had an affair with her boss claimed her husband had never shown her enough love and affection so he had therefore left her "open" to any man who would give her what she'd been without for so many years.

In another instance, a man who became addicted to pornography claimed he had succumbed to the addiction because his wife wasn't "interested enough" in intimacy and thus he lacked fulfillment in that part of his life. He'd therefore had to look for it outside of their marriage. In a third example, another man claimed his wife's demands, her contention and anger—and her blindness to her faults—drove him away from home, where he'd become vulnerable to a woman who'd reached out physically to him. He said he had become receptive to these advances because of how awful his relationship with his wife had become.

As stated previously, after Satan has blinded and deceived transgressors in ways such as this through sexual sin, the journey of regaining the light and discernment of the Savior is an arduous, difficult and lengthy process. It is a step-by-step repentance process that, like forgiveness, will take a great deal of time and effort to achieve. It requires the cleansing and abandonment of sin, humility, obedience, submissiveness and a deep and thorough recognition on the part of transgressors regarding the danger and damage of what they have done to not only themselves but to those around them.

Those transgressors going through this kind of repentance process *never* initially see or recognize the "scales of darkness" (2nd Nephi 30:6) over their eyes or realize the "hardness of their hearts and the blindness of their minds" (1st Nephi 14:7) that are results of their choices and actions. Their thoughts, their rationalizations and the reasoning processes they've adopted because of Satan's influence are not easily recognized, eradicated or overcome. This is where the problems in healing a relationship after sexual sin lie. Transgressors will *always*—inevitably—judge their spouses or others through this tainted thinking. Transgressors often blame them for not being where they should be in their lives, in their relationships, or in the forgiveness process. If ever contention, anger, difficulties, mistrust or other negative emotions or issues arise—and they will, transgressors will often apportion the greatest blame for these problems on their spouses or others, never themselves. Transgressors, too, like the wicked men in King

Noah's court, judge those around them for having judged them. (see Mosiah 13:4) They will blame them for such things as a lack of understanding, the inability to see their own mistakes and weaknesses, as emotionally unstable, as spiritually off base or as not being forgiving or righteous enough. In essence, transgressors always view themselves and where they are at in a much more generous, positive light than those with whom they are working.

For example, one man would always claim his wife would bring in the "spirit of contention" in their discussions whenever she got upset with him about his past choices and tried to point out the damage his sins had done to their relationship. When she expressed her hurt or strong emotion about what he'd done, he would claim that the "contention" she brought in "was not of the Lord." He would therefore refuse to talk with her or work through her feelings, sometimes leaving the room and occasionally turning on her in anger. If she expressed any intense feelings—even if she tried to express herself firmly and without anger, it did not make a difference. Her supposed reactions became his excuse not to discuss the serious issues between the two of them.

In another instance, when one wife would try to explain how her husband's sexual sins were deep, serious and grievous to not only her but the Lord, he would counter her statements with "all men sin" and turn it into a time to remind her of her specific weaknesses and lacks. He acted as if she no right to bring up his sins and the damage done because she, too, was a sinner and had no right to judge him as she did—especially when she never could see clearly her own weaknesses and shortcomings.

As another example, whenever one wife saw her husband interacting with her children in a way she felt would damage them or when she saw other negative behaviors she felt were related to his sins, she would confront him. He would then become angry and claim she used his sins as a "lightning rod" for all the issues that arose between them and in their family. He accused her of "always holding his sins over his head" instead of working through the real issues in their marriage, issues they "would have had whether or not" he had sinned. He would also remind her of all the times she didn't handle parenting or other issues with the same standard she wanted him to uphold and how unfair that was to him.

Because of these types of inaccurate judgments by transgressors, spouses and others outside them must learn to rely on the Savior for what needs to be their truth, perceptions and realities. They must view themselves as the Savior sees them and never view themselves through the eyes of transgressors, especially in relation to the forgiveness process or where they are at in terms of their own personal efforts toward righteousness. This is similar to those Nephites of the church of God who were persecuted because of the "pride" of "their brethren," which "great evil" caused "the more humble part of the people to suffer great persecutions, and to wade through much affliction." They found a key to their wholeness by turning to the Savior. The scriptures say, "They did fast and pray oft, and did wax stronger and stronger in their humility, and firmer and firmer in the faith of Christ, unto the filling their souls with joy and consolation, yea, even to the purifying and the sanctification of their hearts, which sanctification cometh because of their yielding their hearts unto God." (Helaman 3:34-35) They learned to care what God thought, not care what those who were "lifted up in pride" thought. (Helaman 3:34)

Adopting a transgressor's thinking about one's self instead of God's opinions would be similar to Nephi, in the *Book of Mormon,* seeing himself through Laman's and Lemuel's eyes. If Nephi had embraced his brothers' views, he would perceive himself as "lacking in judgment" and "led away by the foolish imaginations of his heart." (1st Nephi 17:19-20) He would see himself as a power-hungry leader who had usurped power and authority, taking the rightful ruling of the people out of his elder brothers' hands. (2nd Nephi 5:3) He would also consider himself a liar who "worketh many things by his cunning arts, that he may deceive." (1st Nephi 16:38) Nephi would have also believed that his words and admonitions arose from "anger" and "sharpness" when he spoke the "word of God, . . .manifesting boldly" concerning his brothers' iniquities. (2nd Nephi 2:26)

Despite Laman's and Lemuel's attacks, their accusations,

their judgments, and their anger and hatred, Nephi never did adopt their views on himself. He never bought into their reality or internalized what they thought of him. He never considered himself perfect—"O wretched man that I am!" (2nd Nephi 4:17)—but he never viewed himself as they did—as evil, contentious, deceptive, spiritually unsound and power-hungry. Nephi did this by never failing to hold onto the Lord's truth, the Lord's strength and the Lord's opinion of him. Nephi said, "I *know* in whom I have trusted. My God has been my support; he hath led me through mine affliction in the wilderness, and he hath preserved me." (2nd Nephi 4:19-20, italics added) Nephi then described where this knowledge and strength came from. He stated, "O Lord, I have trusted in thee, and I will trust in thee *forever*." (2nd Nephi 4:34, italics added)

For those working with transgressors, their skewed "realities" and this type of thinking, strength, hope and insights similar to Nephi's must be gained in order to begin the process of forgiveness. That strength and hope will only come through the Savior, Jesus Christ. If such does not happen, those dealing with transgressors are often beat down relentlessly by transgressors' opinions, attacks, judgments and views. As a result, many have come to taste darkness, despair, depression, discouragement and hopelessness. Many have come to believe they are contentious, vicious, dysfunctional, ugly, fat or of no worth. They often feel they did drive their partners away or that their own weaknesses led to their partners' sins. They may believe they are spiritually off base or mentally or emotionally unstable.

It is only when they can break free of these chains and trust in the Savior and His words, His views and His judgments that they can gain the inward strength and fortitude to become whole and strong in Him. It is only with this wholeness and strength that a person—or a marriage—can even begin to heal.

Two women spoke of their experiences in which they felt that they, too, had suffered from an "addiction"—not to sexual sin but to their partners' good opinions, approval that they could never obtain but which they so desperately wanted. One woman said, "I realized, after my husband's sins came out, that for many years, I had become addicted to trying to please (my husband) and make him happy. I could not stand his disapprobation or displeasure. In fights, I would readily take blame for the contention between us, apologizing for my part in what had happened—even if I didn't feel I was to blame. I would often shed tears afterward, shouldering the burden of his anger and disapproval. I would do whatever I could to make peace between us again. I really couldn't stand for him to be unhappy with me."

She continued, "It took me a long time to break the addiction I had in trying to please him. Even after his sins came out, he would blame me for the majority of contention in our marriage. I would often take it on. I shed countless tears after our arguments, feeling so vulnerable and insecure because he was angry with me. I had to overcome this and learn to wean myself from trying to please him, trying instead to please my Heavenly Father and my Savior. I learned I could not base how I felt about myself on how my husband felt about me or it could destroy me as a person."

Another woman, whose partner left her for someone else, said, "I became obsessed with trying to change (my partner's) views about me. He hated me and blamed me for everything bad in his life. I would often have these intense urges to confront him and try to change his opinions about me—to prove I had loved him and that I had never had ill intentions toward him. I also wanted to prove that I had given the relationship everything I had. Whenever I talked to him, he only hated me more and his views became more set. I couldn't change them. Sometimes I wanted to confront the woman he was with and show her how wrong she was in what she had chosen to do. Caring about them and what they thought put me in terrible anguish and turmoil. It basically incapacitated me in my own life and even resulted in my feeling suicidal—I became so low and discouraged, almost trapped in my desperation. It took me a long time to overcome my depression and try to not care about what either of them thought of me. I slowly overcame my urges to confront them by learning to rely on the Savior. I feel today I've overcome caring about what they think of me. I finally feel free of that obsession."

It should be strongly noted that adopting the Savior's views doesn't necessarily mean those left alone or those working with transgressors believe themselves perfect, without sin and lacking in mistakes, but they do not have to view themselves in the negative light and skewed judgments that transgressors do. They can gain strength about themselves, their lives, their choices, and even their imperfections and mistakes through the Savior's mercy, love, patience and understanding.

One woman described in great depth the process she went through in learning to turn to the Savior—and the Savior alone—to judge where He considered she was at in her life and in the forgiveness process. She described the events and circumstances which led her to realize she had to turn to the Savior for this kind of strength. She began by describing the time when she discovered her husband had a deceptive past, participating in sexual sin throughout almost the whole of their married life. She said:

When I first learned about (my husband's ongoing sexual sins), it was the hardest experience I've ever gone through. I can't adequately describe my misery or my pain. I ached. I was completely devastated. I couldn't believe it was possible that my husband had betrayed me this deeply. I thought he'd loved me and that we were best friends. I thought we had a wonderful partnership—a great marriage. His deception seemed so unreal, almost confusing. He'd lied to me repeatedly. He'd betrayed me—not just once, but a lot. I couldn't figure out why it had happened or know how to deal with it. It was horrible. All of a sudden my husband was someone I didn't know and my marriage was an empty shell, not a relationship valued or treasured or cherished by him.

What was so difficult about this time was I went through tremendous pain for quite awhile—six to seven months, if I had to put a time frame on it. It's not that I got over the pain after that, but I got to a point where I could function better with it. At first, though, I couldn't function at all. My life was a blur. I cried so much. I couldn't eat. I couldn't sleep. I just felt lost so lost and hurting. That time almost seems like a dream, looking back on it now. It still feels unreal. I felt like I couldn't trust anything about my life. Every day I wondered if my husband would go back to his sins, if we'd end up divorcing or if our marriage could ever make it through something that horrific. My heart hurt so much and carried so much pain that sometimes it created actual physical suffering—a hurt I could actually feel inside my heart and chest. I can hardly bear thinking back on that time, even now. I don't feel I could ever go through that kind of pain again.

For the first few months after I'd found out about (my husband), he seemed concerned for me and worried about what he'd done. I think he tried to listen—as much as he could. I'd cry in front of him a great deal. I tried to tell him what I was experiencing and the anguish I was going through, but it was so hard. Here someone I'd turned to before through the trials of my life was the one that was causing me this awful pain. He'd willingly betrayed me and our covenants. I felt so alone.

It was after these first couple of months that things started to change. My husband started to get more and more impatient with me, especially if I tried to bring up his sins or talk about how I felt. I remember one time just sobbing and sobbing in hurt and pain over what had happened. He became angry and frustrated with me, saying things like, "I'm doing everything I can and it isn't enough for you. What more can I do?" He got so angry at that time he said he wondered if he could ever work through all of our issues. This made me feel so shaken and insecure. I felt like he would walk away from our marriage and then blame me for having to leave because of the way I was handling everything.

Here I was suffering with this immense pain and grieving, and it seemed like I couldn't go through the process without getting hurt even further. If I ever got upset when I talked about my husband's sins or how they made me feel, he'd say I had no right to get angry and that he didn't have to work with me when I acted that way. I felt so trapped by my intense emotions on one hand and not being able to work through them on the other. I felt so vulnerable about my life and marriage and frightened that I would lose everything, but I couldn't even work on these difficulties with my husband. I know I didn't handle everything perfectly—who does? But it was as if I didn't have the right to struggle and suffer and hurt and feel the things I did. My husband would say I needed to forgive and learn to love "unconditionally" with the "pure love of Christ," yet I never felt I had access to the same compassion and understanding for my own experiences and suffering.

I've thought about an analogy that helped me put all these feelings into perspective. What I went through is like a person asking someone to stop grieving and feeling pain after a loved one's death. It's like telling them to go through the grieving process in a certain way and in a certain time frame. It's as if someone came up to that person and said, "Get over it. You shouldn't be hurting as much as you are. It's been several months now. You need to stop grieving and feeling sorrow. If you had faith in the atonement of Christ, your pain would go away. You would know your loved one still exists and lives happily with the Savior. Still feeling pain over this loss shows your lack of faith. You need to repent."

In some ways, I felt like I was getting a similar message. "Get over it. Stop hurting and bringing up old issues. Stop feeling the way you do about the past. I'm trying to repent and get my life back in order; you're not seeing all I'm doing to put things right. You need to forgive and love unconditionally. You feel too much anger and contention to perceive things correctly, anyway. All you concentrate on is the mote in my eye and you don't see the beam in your own. You need to change and get over this." I felt like I was getting these same types of messages.

The experience that suddenly made me realize I had to turn completely to the Savior for my strength and support occurred during a particularly rough Sunday. It was a few months after everything had come out and I had ended up sobbing that day—almost in desperation—after something occurred at church which reminded me of our experiences. I wanted to share with my husband the pain I was feeling. I kept trying to describe to him all the uncertainty and darkness—all the turmoil I felt inside. After I'd shared everything with him, I thought he'd be understanding and compassionate. Instead, he said things to me like I was not handling the issues that had come up in my life very well. He said my own problems and the way I was handling things had brought darkness into my life. He said that there were many who had gone through similar trials, but they didn't handle them in the same way I did or suffer like I did. He said I most likely needed outside help and intervention to get over the way I was feeling because it was not right and it stopped me from functioning as I should, that I was not "well."

This is the time I came to realize that I had been doing something that could not be done—trying to get understanding and strength from my husband for what I was experiencing because of his betrayal. It's like I had been hitting my head again and again against a brick wall and I suddenly figured out I needed to stop doing it or I would continue to get hurt by it. My thoughts were, "I'm not emotionally safe or secure in this relationship. My husband does not understand me nor can he at this point; he blames me for the turmoil in our marriage. We don't even have the tools or foundation to come to an understanding. I need to experience what I'm experiencing on my own and work through it myself—without him."

I came to the realization that the only true understanding and strength I could get in my life at that time was from the Savior. I knew I needed Him. I still hurt and felt heartbroken. I didn't know how to live with someone who had hurt me terribly and who didn't know me—and someone I certainly did not know, either, since I'd been so deceived by him in the past. I didn't know if our relationship could work out or if it was going to work out. I didn't feel safe or secure in it. I didn't know how to move forward in our marriage if we did stay together or what I would do if we didn't stay together.

I finally realized that the only thing constant and secure in my life was the Savior. I knew I needed to work on what I was going through with Him and Him alone. I understood that I had to have His love and strength to assure me that I was valued and loved and that my experiences and emotions were valid. I also needed to have the assurance that I was okay in His sight in spite of all my weaknesses and struggles.

This wasn't something I took on and completed instantly. I gained more and more strength by learning to say in my mind, if my husband and I ever fought or disagreed or if he accused me of anything, "The Savior accepts me and He accepts where I am in my life. You may not accept my feelings and experiences, but the Savior does. My emotions and opinions are valid in His eyes. What I'm feeling and experiencing is okay to Him. He will get me through these issues and will work with me, taking me to where I need to go. I will find the right way by turning to Him."

Turning to the Savior like this became the greatest source of strength and comfort I had. I shared with the Savior everything. I gained more confidence and peace in my life, even though the issues between my husband and I were still very difficult—and often volatile.

From the strength I gained from the Savior, it became interesting to see the glimpses of light that came back into our relationship. When I felt more at peace and confident with the Savior, I could handle my husband differently. Instead of getting so uptight about his lack of understanding, I still knew I was understood by Someone and I didn't have to feel anxiety about it. Even if my husband accused me of not handling things the way I should or if he said I didn't understand him, when I knew the Savior accepted where I was at, I didn't feel as threatened or that I needed to prove to my husband that he was wrong about me. I had my own inward confidence from the Savior.

I don't know what will happen in our marriage. There are difficult issues we're still trying to work through and overcome. I do have faith and hope that we can heal if the Savior continues to help us individually. But if we don't heal our relationship, no matter what happens in my life—if my husband does leave, if he does go back to his sins, if we do get a divorce because we can't work through these issues, if I am left alone to care for my children—the Savior will help me. He'll guide me and He'll be with me and He'll walk with me through all of this. He truly is the *only Constant in our lives. Without His strength, I would not have the wholeness that I feel today—despite the issues and challenges that still exist in our marriage.*

All who want to heal marriages and relationships must learn to rely on the Savior for this type of strength. It is only by relying on the Savior's insights and opinions that someone can gain the inward fortitude to overcome deep wounds and begin to forgive. If this does not happen, healing will never occur.

Not only do those working with transgressors need to gain strength from the Savior to work through broken relationships, they need strength like this to deal with the judgments and opinions of others on the outside of those relationships—judgments that will invariably come. Strength and acceptance of where one is at, once again, must come from the Savior and His views and opinions—no one else's. Outside opinions can beat down and thwart in a similar way that transgressors' can—and are often influenced by transgressors. For example, one woman's, Carrie's, own sister turned against her, saying she was a "terrible, neglectful, abusive mother" to her children. Carrie's sister had adopted these judgments from listening to Carrie's husband, who soon after left his marriage for another woman with whom he had an affair.

In another instance, a woman, Heidi, whose husband's extended family "was strong in the church and a very active family," became bitter against Heidi and would no longer associate with her because they "could not believe all the lies she told everyone." They believed the accusations of her ex-husband, their son and brother, despite his affair with another woman.

Another woman told of a experience where she learned this concept even further—relying on the Savior alone for His judgment of where she needed to be—in spite of the fact that the "judgment" came from a "good, faithful man of God, a counselor which my husband and I had worked with for over a year" after her husband's sexual sins were discovered. She describes her experience as follows:

We had been seeing (this counselor) and I had developed trust in his views and opinions. He was an experienced and capable man whom I admired a great deal. Several times I had opened my heart to him, crying in front of him and sharing with him my internal battles. There came a point where my husband and I began seeing him separately for awhile—not together as we had initially.

Some time after this, as I was meeting with this counselor alone, he said to me, in essence, "As I've thought over your circumstances, I don't think you're where you should be in your healing. You have not progressed far enough. I believe this is because you've adopted many ideas that are unsound. You're not humble enough and you don't listen to counsel enough. You're willing to talk about your husband's sins and his issues, but you are not willing to discuss yourself or your own issues. You and I now need to begin to work on you and your issues or you'll never be able to move forward as you should. That's where the problems in your healing lie."

When I went home after meeting with him, I felt broken and crushed. I wept in despair. Was I really all those things he said? Was I really not far enough in my healing because I had adopted "unsound" principles? Was that why I still suffered and felt so much internal misery—because of who I was and the ideas I'd adopted? Is that why our relationship still wasn't healing and moving forward—because of me?

I knelt in prayer to my Heavenly Father, completely broken-hearted. I essentially told Him that I would put everything—my whole soul, my life, my decisions, everything I had become and everything I had done—on the altar. I said to Him, "If I have been wrong, if I have been deceived, if I have adopted ideas that are not in accordance with Thy will, please let me know. I don't want to do anything that takes me away from Thee. I'm willing to open up and change whatever I need to change. Please help me, and please help me know what I need to do."

I asked for a priesthood blessing to bring comfort to me and to help me know what I needed to do at this time. During that blessing, my Heavenly Father assured me that He loved me, that He was proud of me, and that I was where I needed to be in my life. He said if He ever had anything to teach me or chastise me for, He would do it in a way that made me feel determined and peaceful—even if there were things I needed to repent of or learn. He said I would not feel broken-hearted and despairing as I did. He said that He accepted where I was at and that His acceptance was all that mattered. He also told me to trust in that and continue to move forward, knowing He would be with me.

From this experience, I learned that even if there were people I admired whose opinions I trusted and cared about, I still had to accept Heavenly Father's views and opinions over theirs. No one can know of our individual standing before the Lord except the Lord Himself. Others can help influence us for good, it's true— and give insights and try to point the way to Him. But ultimately it is up to me and my Heavenly Father to decide where my standing is before Him.

Laurie Hall in her book *An Affair of the Mind,* describes this idea further. She sets forth a powerful, moving story of what she— a religious Christian woman—went through after her husband's prolonged addiction to pornography and his subsequent multiple encounters with prostitutes. She talked of how people's outside judgments of her during this time were like "flaming arrows" that pierced her wounded heart and soul. She said of her experience:

> When an old family friend heard that Jack and I were separated because he'd been involved in pornography and hookers, she sought to give me some grandmotherly advice.
>
> "I didn't always like sex either, dear," she said, patting my knee. "But I'd pray and ask God to help me and He always would."
>
> There it was. What I just knew people were thinking—*Jack got involved in a sexual addiction because she is a failure in bed.* Earlier a pastor had asked Jack if I had "driven him to it" by withholding myself sexually. This pastor and woman couldn't imagine that "a fine Christian man" would make such choices unless he was driven to it. They couldn't imagine that a

husband would reject his wife sexually.

Later, this same woman gave me a tape on forgiveness and hummed a chorus about how sweet it is to forgive each other. She told me how God hates divorce and implied that if there was a divorce, the fault would be largely mine because I was too hardhearted to forgive. Her implication was that if I would just forgive Jack, everything would magically be all right.

She meant to be helpful, but her helpfulness left me feeling pummeled. She never in any way acknowledged the hurt I was feeling. She never said, "God hates adultery and what's happened to you is wrong." She never dealt with the fact that despite repeated "repentance," Jack had continued in his addiction. No, I was simply counseled to "forgive" and be a better bed partner. Every time I though about what she'd said, it felt like burning in my soul.

She was a kind woman, . . .a simple saint who had been a missionary for over 30 years. Married to a wonderful man, she'd never had to worry about infidelity. She'd had her ups and downs, but she'd never suffered deep injustice and so she had a simplistic answer to my pain.

Neal Clement, director of the American Family Association's OutReach Division, has counseled thousands of sex addicts and their wives. He said, "You can't imagine how many times I've heard from a wife that she was told, 'You need to perform sexually for him.' This kind of advice is abusive. It makes women feel like the answer to his problem lies in her ability to bring him sexual gratification. This is just setting her up for a lot of hurt. It doesn't work and she's left feeling more shame and guilt because she couldn't do it for him.'"

Once you know the truth about your situation and determine to use unchanging principles to guide your response to the nightmare pornography has brought into your home, once you clear your conscience and learn how to build your faith in God, who is able to heal you, you still have another hurdle to overcome—the giant hurdle of other people's judgments of you. Some of these people are genuinely trying to be helpful. Others are genuinely trying to be superior. Either way, when you're hanging by your fingertips to the edge of the abyss of despair, gossip and cutting remarks feel like someone is stomping all over your hands.

Part of the difficulty people have in understanding the devastation of sexual addiction comes from a misunderstanding of what a sex addict looks like and how he behaves in public. At least in the beginning, sex addicts are good at their public persona. I have talked to women whose husbands had a public life as pastors, deacons, lawyers, choir members, youth workers, and other pillars in their community. But privately these men were involved in pornography, and that involvement led them to prostitution, strip shows, homosexuality, and bestiality. Their wives were living in a hell that few people could believe or understand.

We think that someone who is involved in a degenerate lifestyle would have something immediately recognizable about him, like hair growing on his teeth. But police can tell you that the friends and families of serial rapists are often completely incredulous that their loved ones could have done such a thing. And it's not because their friends and families are stupid; it's because pornography so dulls the conscience that their loved ones act like two different people at will.

Because her husband often seems so "normal," the wife of a man with a sexual addiction will have a difficult time finding understanding from others. They are quite sure that the problem can't be as described. So, those passing by her suffering will make judgments. She's too strong for him. She's too weak for him. She's too controlling. She's too passive. She's a dud in bed. She's too demanding in bed. She's stupid for staying in the marriage. She's hardhearted for divorcing him. Everyone will have a different opinion about what she should do and why she finds herself in this situation, and most of the opinions will be whispered behind her back, but not so far behind that she's out of earshot.

Most hurtful of all are the things her husband says in the privacy of their own home: "You drove me to it." "With a wife like you, who wouldn't. . ." "If you would only. . ., I wouldn't have to. . ." "You're too fat." "You're too flat." "You're too old." "Why can't you look like the girl in the picture?" "If you would just dress up a little bit more. . ." "If you weren't so hung up. . ."

. . .No matter whether the source is "helpful" comments made by others or put-downs made by her husband, accusations are like flaming arrows that pierce to the depths of a woman's being. The hurtful comments and disdainful looks feel like they're burning a hole right through her. I think accusation was the most painful part of my ordeal—more painful than the actual betrayal of adultery, more painful than the physical and emotional abuse.

. . .When, despite your best efforts, your dreams are dying before your very eyes, Satan will attack you through thoughts of false guilt and through the judgmental comments of others. People don't even have to say a thing. Their body language can hurl their opinions against you just as easily as their words can. They roll their eyes, they purse their lips, they shake their heads, they cross their arms, they deliberately avoid you. They may not be saying anything, but we know how they feel about us. The disapproval, the condescension, oozes out. You know you've been judged and found wanting.

. . .In Ephesians 6:16, Paul compared false accusations to flaming arrows. I think that's a great analogy because when I got hit by a judgmental comment, it felt like a burning in my soul. (pp. 213-216)

Those who are trying to heal from the repercussions of

sexual sin truly cannot "trust in the arm of flesh" (2ⁿᵈ Nephi 4:24) to get strength and healing but must have the Savior's strength to move forward. As Isaiah powerfully stated, "The Lord Jehovah is my strength and my song; he also has become my salvation." (2ⁿᵈ Nephi 22:2)

5

"If Thou Endure It Well" (D&C 121:8): Struggling through the Process of Healing Damaged Relationships

There are many couples struggling with the repercussions of sexual sin within a relationship that desire and want to move toward healing—if healing is possible. There are some key elements and principles that need to be understood by those trying to rebuild those relationships that are broken and scarred through sexual sin. Those principles are as follows:

There must exist a willingness of both parties to try and rebuild the relationship, a willingness that is not forced or coerced by a partner in the marriage. The willingness of both parties—those who have sinned and those who have been sinned against—to try to move forward in relationships becomes the very first step—the initial key ingredient—of healing relationships damaged by sexual sin. Willingness does not necessarily mean healing and wholeness will occur, but it does put both parties on the path that could lead toward it. However, willingness to try to rebuild cannot be forced, coerced, controlled or manipulated by a partner in the marriage; it must arise from a desire that comes from within.

For many who have been wounded by transgressors, developing willingness to try and heal is an immense, difficult challenge. Sometimes this means one "suffers the will of the Father" (3rd Nephi 11:11) in even attempting to try to move forward in a broken relationship, believing that Heavenly Father desires one to make this step to follow His will. For example, one woman felt tempted again and again to end her marriage following her husband's infidelity, especially as time went on and he still seemed blind to his sins and the damage they had done to her and their children. He continued to find fault with her and blame her for the lacks in their relationship, saying she was unwilling to do anything about them. She became increasingly troubled by her inability to change their circumstances and felt more and more isolated and alone. Each time she would go to the Lord with her concerns and tell Him she wanted to leave, the Lord would ask her to hold on, letting her know that "he knew all things from the beginning" (1st Nephi 9:6) and that He could see much farther than she did. He promised her that He would "take her away" if her husband would never come to cherish and treasure her, but until then, He wanted her to be patient and keep trying, asking her to trust in Him.

Another hardship often occurs while trying to heal damaged relationships. Many times transgressors feel those they've sinned against *owe* them the chance to heal a marriage solely for their desiring it. They essentially demand cooperation by professing it to be the right decision for "our marriage and family." However, as the scriptures say, whenever a covenant has been broken, "even so it has become void and of none effect." (D&C 54:4) When a covenant is dissolved, it becomes a choice by the other party to renew or not to renew, to rebuild or not to rebuild. As the Lord has said, "Unto every law there are certain bounds also and conditions. All beings who abide not in those conditions are not justified." (D&C 88:39)

Manipulating spouses to try and force them to work on the relationship, then, to ask them to forgive or love unconditionally because that is what they should do will not work. Transgressors must understand that a renewed desire to continue forward will only come from their own fruits of righteousness—that is, true humility, deep and thorough repentance, and their "striving to repair all the injuries which they ha(ve) done" (Mosiah 27:35) because of their destructive choices. The Lord has said, "If he confess his sins before thee and me, *and repenteth in the sincerity of his heart*, him shall ye forgive, and I will forgive him also." (Mosiah 26:29, italics added) This "sincerity of heart" is imperative and includes humility and a thorough determination to repent and change.

Furthermore, when transgressors become able to view their spouses' willingness to try again in a marriage after they have destroyed it as a privilege instead of an expectation, changes in their approach to their partners will often escalate the healing process instead of damaging it through demands, control or manipulation.

It should be remembered that when transgressors do not change or give up sinful habits, the Lord does not expect their spouses to stay in destructive relationships. The prophet Jacob, when talking to adulterous men who had hurt their wives and children, warned them, "The time speedily cometh, that except ye repent. . .*the Lord God will lead away the righteous out from among you*." (Jacob 3:4, italics added) He "will not suffer their cries any longer" (Mormon 8:41) but will "make a way for (their) escape." (D&C 132:50) The Lord will lead someone away from a relationship if behaviors and sins do not change. He does not expect someone to live in a relationship that, as James E. Faust has described it, has become "a prolonged and apparently irredeemable relationship which is destructive of a person's dignity as a human being." (*Ensign*, May 1993, p. 36) The Lord said it this way:

> I, the Lord, have seen the sorrow, and heard the mourning of the daughters of my people. . .because of the wickedness and abominations of their husbands.
>
> And I will not suffer, saith the Lord of Hosts, that the cries of the fair daughters of this people. . .shall come up unto me against the men of my people, saith the Lord of Hosts.

> For they shall not lead away captive the daughters of my people because of their tenderness, save I shall visit them with a sore curse, even unto destruction. (Jacob 2:31-33)

It should be noted there are many who will never be given the opportunity to try and rebuild a marriage after sexual sin has been present in a relationship. This is because many transgressors choose to leave a marriage and continue in their sins, intent on the courses they have chosen. When this happens, those who have been left behind by transgressors should never take the blame for the relationship disintegrating. Almost without fail, transgressors will try to lay blame for their choices at their spouses' feet. But, as Boyd K. Packer once stated, "Some marriages have broken up in spite of all that one partner could do to hold the marriage together. While there may be faults on both sides, I do not condemn the innocent one who suffers in spite of all that was desired and done to save the marriage." (*Ensign,* May 1981, p. 14)

Healing a broken marriage and relationship takes a great deal of time—time that is measured in months and years, not days and weeks. One of the most difficult aspects of healing relationships marred by sexual sin is the great amount of time needed to even begin the process of moving forward. When sexual sin has occurred in a marriage, the old relationship is destroyed and must be built again "on a rock"—those eternal principles that are immovable—and not "upon the sand" (3rd Nephi 26:27)—the shaky foundation the marriage and relationship had been built on previously. This is a lengthy process that takes extensive time. It entails the cleansing of sin and a "mighty change" of heart (Alma 5:12) by transgressors. For those who have been hurt by them, it is a process of learning to deal with the pain of a betrayal and then move beyond it to forgive deep wounds received. Moving forward also includes replacing old patterns and ways of relating with new ones; it includes sincere and prolonged efforts to overcome contention, anger, judgments and other difficulties that will inevitably arise after sin has been present.

One woman said, "One of the most sobering realities about finding out about my husband's sexual sins was that our marriage was not okay. It pained me to realize we had dysfunction in our relationship—not only because of my husband's sins but because of my living with them and around them for so long, accepting the difficulties that arose from them as a normal part of life. As we've tried to move forward in our relationship and heal our marriage, the dysfunction between us has become even more apparent. We don't have the tools to work together and we're having to learn those tools. It's very difficult and hard—and has resulted in many tears, many fights and countless misunderstandings. It's a long road and I know it's going to take a long time to traverse it." This becomes true for any trying to heal.

Many counselors and others have adopted the idea that "it takes a year" to even begin the process of healing. That means, in essence, that the first part of healing relationships doesn't include actual healing at all. It usually is a complex dilemma of juggling with individual concerns, trying to work through them before being able to work on the relationship together. Transgressors must struggle with overcoming sins and weaknesses while victims must deal with their pain, wounds, and hurts from betrayals. Only when both sides can begin to deal effectively with these individual matters with the Savior will either move toward the capacity to repair the damage that has been done between them. Repairing damage includes working through intense issues and deep emotions which often result in misunderstandings, contention, anger, blame and so forth. Only those willing to commit to the great length of time it takes to overcome all of these obstacles will even have the chance to move toward healing.

Transgressors must overcome the snare of pride; victims must escape the trap of pain. Another essential step in moving toward healing a relationship is twofold: Transgressors must overcome the pride that has been a part of their lives, and victims must learn not to become trapped by the pain that has come to them because of the choices of others.

For transgressors, this means that they must learn that

their views, judgments and ways of relating have been damaged by dark influences allowed in because of their sins. Because of this damage, they must be willing to acknowledge their hearts and minds have been affected, resulting in skewed thinking and faulty reasoning. In essence, transgressors must learn that they can't trust themselves, their opinions or their views completely. It is only when the light of Christ is allowed into their lives in greater and greater abundance that they will be able to discern correctly. It is then that they will come to realize in greater degrees that Christ has had to awaken them "out of a deep sleep" (Alma 5:7) to teach them new and different realities, realities based on His truths, His teachings and His doctrine. Until this comes about, transgressors need to humbly accept that they have much to learn and overcome.

Those who have been hurt by transgressors will experience suffering and pain because of betrayals and wrong choices made by transgressors. Grief and suffering are inevitable byproducts of betrayals and are not bad but necessary to experience in order to move beyond them. Most spouses who have been betrayed have gone through a grieving pattern similar to those who have suffered from a death; they struggle with shock, anger, fear, uncertainty, anguish and turmoil—many intense emotions that will take a great deal of time to experience and overcome.

There are two ways those who have been hurt by sexual sin can become trapped by their pain. The first occurs when victims don't acknowledge, work through or allow themselves to feel the hurtful emotions others have caused them. In doing this, those wounded come to stifle all of their emotions and feelings, handicapping themselves in other areas of their lives.

One woman tried to describe what happened when she dealt with her pain by burying it and trying to ignore it. She said how she "wouldn't let herself cry" or let the pain come into her heart after she found out about her husband's sins; dealing with her emotions felt too frightening and daunting. She therefore tried to become immune to them—letting herself become cold and unfeeling instead of hurting and suffering because of what had happened. In doing this, however, she eventually—after some time—came to see that she had not only killed her pain, she had stifled her ability to feel and experience emotions in other areas of her life. She felt impaired in loving her children deeply and freely; she became cold and contentious in her interactions with other people; she and her husband's relationship became a "co-existent" relationship where they worked around each other, not together or with each other to overcome what had happened.

Finally, when this woman learned to see what she had done, she allowed herself to "re-experience" the grieving process. Tears and hurtful memories became a part of this, but she felt through this that she regained her ability to feel and work through her buried emotions. She felt she could thus overcome them instead of becoming trapped by them, where they still hurt and cankered her soul, not disappearing as she had hoped—or thought—they would.

Another way those who have been hurt become trapped by their pain is to experience that pain again and again, never letting it go. Emotions felt from betrayals are deep and they are real. However, the adversary is a master at inflicting even deeper and more extensive pain. He will play upon the wounds and hurts received and wound even further, causing further turmoil, deeper wounds and more intense suffering. He brings up images incessantly in the minds of victims, reminding them of what their spouses have done, replaying their actions and betrayals over and over in their minds. He whispers such things as, "Your spouse betrayed you. You are not valued and loved. You mean nothing for someone to do this to you. Think of this; remember what he or she has done. Picture it again and again. See? See how you are not valued and loved? See how you are a nothing in your spouse's eyes? See how little he or she thought of you and your covenants? Feel that hurt; let that pain penetrate your heart. Relive it again and again. You are a nothing because of what has happened to you. Remember, remember, remember."

Those who have been wounded must learn to fight these incessant thoughts and memories from the adversary just as transgressors have to fight bad thoughts and memories. When the hurts and pains are re-lived, re-experienced and reviewed over and over again, the pain and grief can become immobilizing and stop eternal progress.

One woman described how her mother, whose husband had left her, still relived the emotions of her betrayal every single day—despite the fact that over four years had passed since he had left for another woman. Each day she would allow memories that would bring up her immense pain. She would cry, feel fully the grief as if it was new, and then become caught in the quagmire of her emotions. From this, her mother felt great fatigue, could hardly function in other areas of her life, and became unable to move forward and heal. She allowed her mind to dwell incessantly on the injuries and hurts she'd received.

Another woman spoke about how the Savior helped her learn to replace the hurtful thoughts Satan would try to give her with His thoughts. Many times whenever Satan would begin to draw her mind to the past, her husband's betrayal and his leaving her, the Lord would gently admonish her through His Spirit, "No; let's remove those thoughts. Let's replace them with something different." He would then help remind her of scriptures, conference talks, hymns or perhaps loving gestures by others that He had sent to help her through her grieving process. Sometimes the Lord would bring up promises from priesthood blessings she'd been given, particularly the promise that one day she would be given someone who loved and cherished her and would throughout eternity. By learning to replace the adversary's thoughts with the Lord's thoughts, she felt herself moving toward healing and wholeness instead of becoming trapped by Satan's darkness.

As mentioned in the previous chapter, another way of overcoming the pain of betrayal is learning to trust the Lord's perceptions and views about one's own self instead of adopting the views of a transgressor or the adversary. Whereas a transgressor or the adversary might have someone view a betrayal as a reflection on his or her offering as a spouse caused by personal lacks, faults or weaknesses, the Savior would counter otherwise.

He would have someone understand that each must work out his or her "own individual salvation with fear and trembling before him," (Mormon 9:28) not blaming or putting the responsibility on someone else. The Savior would also have someone wounded understand that he or she is a valued son or daughter of God, one loved, one treasured, one whom He will never forsake and abandon, and one whom He can entreat and succor because He has felt every wound, experienced every emotion and every particle of that son's or daughter's life. Learning to rely on the Savior and His views will become a natural shield against the deeper wounds and pain the adversary will try to inflict on those who have already been wounded. As with everything in this life, the Savior becomes the true key to healing and wholeness.

The overcoming of sinful practices does not constitute complete "healing"; solely choosing to stay together does not constitute "healing." Oftentimes transgressors feel that if they have been able to overcome sin in their lives, such becomes sufficient for their offerings toward their efforts to heal a marriage. However, President Ezra Taft Benson taught,

> Repentance means more than simply a reformation of behavior. Many men and women in the world demonstrate great will-power and self-discipline in overcoming bad habits and the weaknesses of the flesh. Yet at the same time they give no thought to the Master, sometimes even openly rejecting Him. Such changes of behavior, even if in a positive direction, do not constitute true repentance.
> . . .True repentance is based on and flows from faith in the Lord Jesus Christ. There is no other way. True repentance involves *a change of heart and not just a change of behavior* (see Alma 5:13). (*The Teachings of Ezra Taft Benson,* p. 71, italics added)

This "change of heart" is a complete change of life—of thought patterns, choices, habits, ways of relating, ways of serving, ways of showing and giving love, and so forth. Often transgressors feel if they've overcome their sins, everything else and everyone around them should be okay. A change of heart, however, entails repairing, rebuilding and correcting mistakes of the past. It is the willingness to acknowledge the damage choices have done and then help others heal from the damage done. Healing a marriage comes through this change of heart, not through solely overcoming grievous habits or mistakes.

Another aspect of healing is realizing that staying together in a marriage after a betrayal has occurred does not constitute healing. If "staying together" moves a couple toward renewed love, growing trust, increased hope and strength, forgiveness and repentance, that constitutes true healing. This will not come about solely because of the decision to "stick with it for the children" or for other reasons. Healing takes effort, tears, prayers, determination and most of all the strength and insights of the Savior, who is the only One from whom true healing flows.

There is another aspect to healing a marriage that should be discussed. Often those who have been wounded by transgressors will feel directed of the Lord to stay within a marriage to work on it; they feel the Lord's directive to cultivate the willingness to continue attempts to forgive and heal. Many times, however, after these sincere attempts, transgressors will still leave a marriage. Transgressors may claim, for instance, that they "could never continue to live with this terrible relationship" or with an awful spouse who "doesn't love or understand" them enough. They may refuse to deal with "someone who just can't get over this" or who can't work through issues or accept their efforts toward healing.

Many wonder why the Lord would allow them to go through further hurt, heartache and pain solely to have their spouses leave and their marriages end. They may wonder why the Lord would have directed them to stay and try to move forward when He knew ultimately the relationship would fail. Often the Lord allows us to learn through pain and trials some of the deepest lessons possible in this life, lessons that can't be learned any other way. Those hurt like this often come to realize on a deep, penetrating level—deeper than many—that they can only get true wholeness and complete healing from the Savior, not from anyone or anything outside themselves. They come to learn to base their wholeness, security, strength, well-being and happiness on the Savior, His light, His peace, His grace and His power. Those injured must trust that if the Savior did direct them to stay, He had reasons that would "give the(m) experience, and shall be for th(eir) good." (D&C 121:7)

Orson F. Whitney has said,

> No pain that we suffer, no trial that we experience is wasted. It ministers to our education, to the development of such qualities as patience, faith, fortitude and humility. All that we suffer and all that we endure, especially when we endure it patiently, builds up our characters, purifies our hearts, expands our souls, and makes us more tender and charitable, more worthy to be called the children of God. . .and it is through sorrow and suffering, toil and tribulation, that we gain the education that we came here to acquire and which will make us more like our Father and Mother in heaven. (*Improvement Era,* March 1966, p. 211)

One woman, who had to experience much darkness and many trials in her life because of her husband's betrayal, said that what she went through "made her so much less judgmental of others than I used to be. When I see others struggle with depression or discouragement, instead of being critical I wonder what they're going through and how I can help. When I heard that someone I knew attempted suicide, I only felt to mourn for the pain she felt that could leave her so desperate. Heavenly Father has taught me through my adversity how to be more compassionate and caring of others instead of being critical and distant. I feel I've learned to love better and more deeply than I used to love."

There is a final point that needs to be made in relation to marriages not healing after the Lord has directed an injured spouse to stay in a marriage and work on it. Many times the Savior will allow transgressors the chance to heal and if they don't take it and decide to leave, "that they may do this thing unto (their spouses), according to the hardness of their hearts, that the judgments which he shall exercise upon them in his wrath may be just." (Alma 14:11) Many transgressors do not realize "that it was the Lord that had spared them, and granted unto them a chance for repentance" (Mormon 3:3) and that they didn't take it, thus opening themselves up to His judgment. The Lord promises he will "mete out a just recompense upon the heads of all their oppressors." (D&C 127:3)

All people make mistakes; however, some of those mistakes can literally destroy a marriage. All mistakes are not equal. Often in attempts to heal relationships, transgressors will be sure to point out all the foibles, weaknesses and faults of their partners, claiming they are not perfect and therefore as much responsible for the problems, contention and difficulties in their marriages. This is not true. No one is without sin in this existence, but all sins are not equal. In the Lord's eyes, sexual transgression is second only to murder. It cannot even begin to compare with minor offenses spouses may return in their efforts to work through difficulties that have arisen in marriages because of betrayals. As one Bishop explained it, sexual sins are "telestial" mistakes that can literally destroy; the other mistakes are "terrestrial" mistakes that are easily forgivable and overlooked by all who are part of healthy marriages.

Until transgressors realize they must accept the greater portion of blame and responsibility for damages done to their marriages—for the blame, anger, contention, mistrust, hurt and other struggles that abound, they will usually continue to criticize, condemn and point out incessantly the weaknesses of their partners, shifting the majority of the blame for marital problems to them. The weaknesses of their partners often become the excuse for transgressors to withdraw from working with them—which may include even leaving a marriage—or from transgressors' further attempts to try and heal relationships. Accountability, in essence, is shifted by transgressors to their partners for where relationships are at in terms of healing; they do not accept it as their own or as arising from their choices and actions. It is only when transgressors take complete accountability for the seriousness of their mistakes—instead of comparing them to others'—that relationships can begin to heal.

There are powerful, cunning forces at work against a marriage; only with the Lord will those be discerned and overcome. Many couples stand in literal awe at the forces that work against them and their marriages after sexual sin has been present therein. Satan and his forces work on transgressors; those forces work on the innocent souls surrounding transgressors; even those closely associated with them are often targeted. The traps, barbs, the "mighty winds, yea, (the) shafts in the whirlwind, . . .the hail and mighty storm" (Helaman 5:12) that come from Satanic attacks can be frightening, daunting, overwhelming and sometimes overpowering.

Laurie Hall stated, in her book *An Affair of the Mind,* that she "finally had to accept that somehow, in some way, the spirit forces of wickedness have access to a family in which the father is involved in pornography. Until I was willing to accept this, I was fighting a losing battle because I was trying to respond to what was happening as if I were dealing with things I could see and touch."

She continues, "Once I accepted that I was dealing with something beyond the realm of the physical, I had a whole new war chest of weapons to handle the situation. These new weapons helped me find peace in the midst of the storm." (p. 121)

It cannot be overstated that only those who have the light and guidance of the Savior can withstand the clever, cunning attacks of Satan and his forces. As Marion G. Romney once said, "Satan is evil: totally and always. He ever seeks to defeat the gospel plan and 'destroy the souls of men' (D&C 10:27). . . .Satan's methods are various, devious, and countless." He then quotes Joseph S. Smith, who stated, "By every possible means (Satan) seeks to darken the minds of men and then offers them falsehood and deception in the guise of truth. Satan is a skillful imitator. . . .(As) the 'father of lies' he has. . .become, through the ages of practice in his nefarious work, such an adept 'that were it possible he would deceive the very elect.'" (*Ensign,* Feb. 2005, pp. 54-55).

So much of overcoming sexual sin entails seeing Satan for the cunning, powerful and skillful master that he is. Then it is only by turning to the true Master for His sustaining strength can evil forces be discerned and overcome.

As pointed out previously, there are many complex and deep issues surrounding the process of healing a marriage. The above principles and points can become a starting ground for attempts to move forward toward healing, but that's all they are—a starting ground. The process of healing is indeed a lengthy, time-consuming process that will take the "merits, and mercy, and grace of the Holy Messiah." (2nd Nephi 2:8) As Dallin H. Oaks once said, "God's mercy is the only source of the ultimate and eternal joy, which restores every loss, dries every tear, and erases every pain." (*Ensign,* Nov. 1991, p. 74)

6

"The Arms of Mercy Are Extended Towards Them" (Alma 5:33)

Another aspect that can help a marriage and relationship move toward forgiveness and healing occurs when those who have been wounded begin to develop compassion for the plight of transgressors—those people who have hurt or betrayed them through sexual sin. This compassion can only come from a position of strength that is a result of, as mentioned earlier, having the light and strength of the Savior that comes from adopting His views, His opinions and His insights about themselves. Through this strength, victims may often begin to look outside their own pain and become instruments of healing and strength for transgressors in their pain—that is, if transgressors are humble and willing to accept help, not if they are hard of heart, unrepentant, or unwilling to change. Once again, this can occur *only* if those wounded have the strength of the Savior to help sustain them and *only* if transgressors are humble and willing to be helped.

First off, it needs to be understood that transgressors have essentially sought for "something which (they) could not obtain." They have "sought for happiness in doing iniquity, which thing is contrary to the nature of that righteousness which is in our great and Eternal head." (Helaman 13:38) Though there are some who are led down the paths of sin because of poor and unwise choices, many transgressors sin because they are looking to fulfill deep and unmet personal needs inside them. These needs often come because of lacks from their pasts—from not having unconditional love during childhood, for example, or for expectations—of themselves or others—they felt they could never meet. Many have been victims of abuse, abandonment or neglect. So often transgressors have grown up in homes where sin has been present and they have been exposed to the repercussions of the unrighteous choices of others—fathers or others in the home who have influenced them. As James E. Talmage said in the *Articles of Faith,* "Good and evil tendencies, blessings and curses, are transmitted from generation to generation." (p. 87)

For example, two brothers who grappled with pornography addictions found out many years later that throughout their lives, their father had struggled with an ongoing deep pornography addiction, as well. They were both victims of his mean and unyielding temper, and they both felt they could "never live up" to his rigid expectations of them. Despite attempts to succeed in their own lives and their efforts to try and please him, they were never able to do so and lived constantly with his disapprobation.

As another example, one man who battled a deep sexual addiction grew up in a home where his father had participated in an affair during his formative years. Though his father tried to repent, his father's decisions rocked the foundation of love and security in their home for many years. This man basically grew up with a father consumed with himself and one who had neglected his family, paying no heed to his children's individual concerns.

In summary, transgressors have often made poor choices because they were looking to satisfy internal thirsts of their own, seeking to quench them by drinking from poisoned wells—drinks that only hurt and harmed them further and never brought the desired wholeness they were looking to find. Many have followed "forbidden paths" (1ˢᵗ Nephi 8:28) because they have been "blinded by the subtle craftiness of men" (D&C 123:7) whose intent was to "lie in wait to destroy." (D&C 5:32) Through their choices, they have wounded themselves more grievously and have brought in guilt, shame, the loss of the spirit, deeper hurts and more extensive wounds, "hardness of their hearts and blindness of their minds," (Alma 13:4) the inability to give love and receive love as the Lord intended, and finally the buffetings of Satan and the influence of his dark spirits.

Because of this, transgressors' further suffering is inevitable. It is a condition and law of mortality. As Richard G. Scott has said, "Trials, disappointments, sadness, and heartache come to us from two basically different sources. *Those who transgress the laws of God will always have those challenges.* The other reason for adversity is to accomplish the Lord's own purposes in our lives." (*Ensign,* Nov. 1995, p. 16, italics added) As the Lord stated in the *Doctrine & Covenants,* "They were found transgressors, therefore they must needs be chastened." (101:41) Knowing transgressors will and must suffer can produce feelings of compassion and concern for them, even when they continue to harm and hurt those around them. Though transgressors experience "joy in their works for a season, . . .by and by the end cometh" (3rd Nephi 27:11) and they will reap the bitter fruits of their choices.

Transgressors' sorrow and suffering come from many different sources. They may occur in such things as hardships in careers or personal relationships; financial difficulties; health problems or challenges; and a myriad of other temporal challenges and difficulties. Spiritual confusion, unrest, discouragement, depression, hopelessness and despair are inevitable fruits because "despair cometh because of iniquity." (Moroni 10:22) Loneliness, isolation, feeling socially shunned or rejected, feeling the loss of self-worth and self-respect, self-hatred and self-loathing are common afflictions, as well—even if transgressors maintain relationships of sin with others. As Neal A. Maxwell stated pertaining to this,

Henry Fairlie has written perceptively in his book *The Seven Deadly Sins Today* concerning how "the lustful person will usually be found to have a terrible hollowness at the center of his life" and about "the desert he has made of himself and his life." (p.187) "Lust," wrote Fairlie, "is not interested in its partners, but only in the gratification of its own craving. Lust dies at the next dawn, and when it returns in the evening, to search where it may, it is with its own past erased." (p. 175)

Those so drained by sensuality do, in fact, seek to compensate for their loneliness by sensations. However, in the arithmetic of appetite, anything multiplied by zero still totals zero! But the senseless search goes on. . . .

So it is that sexual immorality finally causes the isolation of the individual from God, from others, and yes, even from oneself! (*Young Adult Fireside on Temple Square*, June, 1985)

Truly, loneliness and isolation are inescapable afflictions that will come to transgressors, even if outside relationships are maintained. Since it is often "by the wicked that the wicked are punished," (Mormon 4:5) many times these outside relationships will be the cause of more extensive heartache, trials and suffering for transgressors, as well.

Suffering and sorrow also come as transgressors lose more and more control over their lives and their abilities to govern them. Sometimes the bonds of sin become so deep they literally trap souls in darkness and misery. These shackles are not easily overcome. Sterling W. Sill spoke about these kinds of traps when he stated, "Many thousands of people are living a tortured existence. . . .Attached to some thousands of individuals is some galling, oppressive handicap which is sapping their energy, exhausting their mental and spiritual resources, and depleting their ability to live happy, productive lives. They are compelled to carry each newly acquired torment with them wherever they go until eventually, exhausted and defeated, they give up the struggle into some part of the sea of discouragement, failure, and death." (*New Era,* Oct. 1976, p. 5) It is painful, tortuous work for transgressors to "shake off the awful chains by which (they) are bound" (2nd Nephi 1:13) and become clean, pure and whole again through repentance, a process characterized by deep and intense pain and suffering. Bruce R. McConkie stated, "Sometimes the spiritual struggle to slay sin. . .is as savage a warfare as death by crucifixion." (*Promised Messiah,* p. 389) Suffering, then, is an innate part of overcoming the enslaving bondage sin invariably brings.

Finally, suffering and afflictions will come to transgressors from the buffetings of Satan and his minions in which those dark spirits are given the chance to afflict and torment, even to the point of emotional or mental pain and spiritual agony, turmoil and anguish. As it says in the scriptures, "Verily, verily I say unto you, if a man marry a wife according to my word. . .and he or she shall commit any sin or transgression of the new and everlasting covenant whatever, . . .they shall be destroyed in the flesh, and shall be delivered unto the buffetings of Satan unto the day of redemption, saith the Lord God." (D&C 132:26) Dallin H. Oaks summarized this by saying,

> Those who yield to the enticing of Satan may, as the scripture says, "enjoy the pleasures of sin for a season" (Heb. 11:25), but that kind of pleasure can never lead to lasting happiness or eternal joy. The spirit and influence of Satan bring feelings of confusion, contention, darkness, disorder, anger, hate, and misery. Persons who pursue Satan's way are certain to have Satan's misery. Unless they repent they will "remain with the father of lies, in misery, like unto himself." (*Ensign,* Nov. 1991, p. 75)

Philip A. Harrison, in his book *Clean Hands, Pure Heart*— a book describing his attempts to overcome a deep and prolonged pornography addiction, described it this way. He said,

I have heard of insanity being defined as "*doing
the same thing over and over again, hoping for a
different result*." What better description could be found
for the endlessly repeating cycle I was caught in for
most of my life—acting out, then suffering inevitable
demoralization? Over and over I asked, "Why do I keep
hurting myself this way? It just doesn't make sense to
keep doing something that, in the end, always brings
such sorrow and despair!" However, my thinking *was*
"insane," because I just kept saying to myself, "Maybe
this time I can get away with it. Maybe this time I will
only have the rush and not the guilt. Maybe this time,
wickedness *will* be happiness!" I might just as well
have jumped off a building and hoped I would fall *up*.
(p. 60)

Although suffering like this is inevitable, often suffering,
agony and misery don't seem to display themselves until many,
many years after transgressors have chosen their paths of sin. For
example, one man left his wife and five children after a sustained
adulterous relationship with another woman. He and that woman
later married and were together for several years. After the
adulterous relationship eventually ended and the man was left
alone, one of his children came to him and asked him, "Dad, how
do you feel now after all that's happened? What is it like for you
to live with your choices of the past?" He soberly responded, "It's
like waking up to death every day." He had a thorough and heavy
knowledge of what his sins had done to him, his family, friends
and other loved ones, and his repentance process was sore and
grievous—resulting in much inward suffering and turmoil.

In another instance, one man's eventual suffering came
when he saw many of his children taking paths similar to what
he had chosen. One child had a prolonged affair and divorced a
spouse; others had become addicted to pornography. Some were
unfaithful in their relationships or had spouses that were unfaithful
to them. Further sorrow came to him when he saw the devastating
fruits of sexual sin in his own family.

It should be taken into account that sometimes the suffering of transgressors will not become manifest in this life. One man left his wife and family for another woman, abandoning them entirely. He withdrew completely from the lives of his children and grandchildren, claiming, "My children are grown now; I've done my work with them. It's time for me to live my own life." He never renewed relationships or tried to repent. Though his family has never seen the suffering that comes from sin, the Lord has stated, "Hypocrites shall be cut off, either in life or in death, even as I will." (D&C 50:8) Each will be "brought before the bar of God, to be judged of our works." Then, as the scriptures further tell us,

> If our hearts have been hardened, yea, if we have hardened our hearts against the word, insomuch that it has not been found in us, then will our state be awful, for then we shall be condemned.
>
> For our words will condemn us, yea, all our works will condemn us; we shall not be found spotless; and our thoughts will also condemn us; and in this awful state we shall not dare to look up to our God; and we would fain be glad if we could command the rocks and the mountains to fall upon us to hide us from his presence.
>
> But this cannot be; we must come forth and stand before him in his glory, and in his power, and in his might, majesty, and dominion, and acknowledge to our everlasting shame that all his judgments are just. (Alma 12:12-15)

The Lord also warns:

> I command you to repent—repent, lest I smite you by the rod of my mouth, and by my wrath, and by my anger, and your sufferings be sore—how sore you know not, how exquisite you know not, yea, how hard to bear you know not.

For behold, I, God, have suffered these things for all, that they might not suffer if they would repent;

But if they would not repent they must suffer even as I;

Which suffering caused myself, even God, the greatest of all, to tremble because of pain, and to bleed at every pore, and to suffer both body and spirit.

. . .Wherefore, I command you again to repent, lest I humble you with my almighty power; and that you confess your sins, lest you suffer these punishments of which I have spoken. (D&C 19:15-20)

Knowing that transgressors will and must suffer "much anguish of soul because of their iniquities" (Mosiah 28:4) can instill a deep and earnest desire in those they have hurt to be compassionate towards them and their plight. Those wounded like this can become of the sons of Mosiah who "could not bear that any human soul should perish; yea, even the very thought that any soul should endure endless torment did cause them to quake and tremble." (Mosiah 27:3) This compassion can move those harmed toward prayers of faith in transgressors' behalf that they may become whole, clean and healed of their deep personal wounds through the Savior. If transgressors become willing and humble, then this compassion can even become the impetus which can help those hurt to be supportive, caring and helpful in the process of overcoming the painful effects of transgression. "Pray ye, therefore, that their ears may be opened unto your cries, that I may be merciful unto them, that these things may not come upon them," (D&C 101:92) the Lord tells us.

One woman told of an incident that helped her gain compassion for the circumstances her husband had put her and himself in because of his deep sexual sin. Because of his being exposed to pornography as a young teen, he had developed a prolonged addiction which had led him to multiple times of unfaithfulness. This woman said, "One day I was carrying the burdens of all that I had to go through because of my husband's choices. I felt so angry and defeated. I'd had to go through so much turmoil and heartache! It seemed unfair. I said to Heavenly Father, 'It's so unfair that you've made me go through this. It's so unfair that my husband put me through this.' The Lord gently whispered back to me, 'It's unfair that (your husband) was exposed to pornography as a young boy.'" This woman came to understand that many of her husband's sins had occurred because of unfair things that had happened to him, and it gave her a greater sense of compassion for his struggles and weaknesses.

"It's a Bigger Problem Than We Know"

One bishop, in expressing to his ward council the dangers and damages of sexual sin that had occurred within his stewardship, expressed with great soberness and sorrow, "It's a bigger problem than we know." Part of effectively dealing with transgressors is learning to understand how pervasive and widespread sexual sin has become.

Laurie Hall in her book *An Affair of the Mind* said that after her book came out, she "spent a number of years in active ministry" helping others who had gone through what she had experienced because of her husband's pornography addiction and subsequent adultery. She described how pervasive sexual sin had become throughout the families of those she had worked with. She said:

> During those years (of ministry), I was a guest on more than 200 radio and television programs, traveled thousands of miles, spoke to tens of thousands of people, listened to hundreds of confessions, and held many sobbing men and women in my arms. I discovered that pornography is a bigger problem than I thought it was when I first wrote my book. Several different studies show that anywhere from 40 to 50 percent of married Christian men are masturbating to pornography. It is scarcely possible to overstate the problem. It's not just the guy in the pew who's struggling—many pastors, youth leaders, and worship ministers are also caught in

porn's clutches.

That means that on any given Sunday morning, at least half the families in your average congregation are battling this hidden enemy of marriage. (p. 248)

It can be assumed that many in Latter-day Saint congregations are struggling in similar ways—not with just pornography but other sexual sins, as well. Many in ecclesiastical leadership positions are not immune, either. In one support group that a man attended while dealing with his sexual addiction, he became acquainted with a recently-released bishop and also a previous stake president who were there for the same reasons.

Another bishop developed a pornography addiction when he wanted to "see what (a member of his congregation) was struggling with so I could better help him." But by partaking of that poison, he, too, became poisoned and addicted.

Sexual sin truly is becoming rampant and cannot be ignored as inconsequential. President Hinckley, in the October 2004 General Conference, described how sexual sin is becoming a "raging storm, destroying individuals and families, utterly ruining what was once wholesome and beautiful." Though he is speaking of "pornography in all of its manifestations" when he said this, it could certainly include any type of sexual sin. (*Ensign,* Nov. 2004, p. 59)

"Ye Were Made Sorry After a Godly Manner"—(1st Corinthians 5:1)—A Necessary Step Toward True Repentance

Spencer W. Kimball once said, "We must remember that repentance is more than just saying, 'I am sorry.' It is more than tears in one's eyes. It is more than a half a dozen prayers. *Repentance means suffering. If a person hasn't suffered, he hasn't repented.* I don't care how many times he says he has. If he hasn't suffered, he hasn't repented. He has got to go through a change in his system whereby he suffers and then forgiveness is a possibility." (*Teachings of Spencer W. Kimball,* p. 99, italics added)

Truly, suffering is an inevitable byproduct of sin. The Savior chastens those He loves—that is, He allows suffering, hardships, afflictions and difficulties—"that their sins may be forgiven, for with the chastisement I prepare a way for their deliverance in all things out of temptation, and I have loved you." (D&C 95:1) Adversities are given to transgressors, then, that they might develop the type of sorrow that moves them toward repentance, for a "man sometimes, if he is compelled to be humble, seeketh repentance; and now surely, whosoever repenteth shall find mercy." (Alma 32:13) This sorrow is far different than the sorrow the Nephites displayed before their final destruction, for "their sorrowing was not unto repentance, because of the goodness of God; but it was rather the sorrowing of the damned, because the Lord would not always suffer them to take happiness in sin. . . .They did not come unto Jesus with broken hearts and contrite spirits, but they did curse God, and wish to die." (Mormon 2:13-14)

The only kind of sorrow that will ultimately save a transgressor from spiritual death is defined by Ezra Taft Benson as "godly sorrow." He describes it as "a gift of the Spirit. It is a deep realization that our actions have offended our Father and our God. It is the sharp and keen awareness that our behavior caused the Savior, He who knew no sin, even the greatest of all, to endure agony and suffering. Our sins caused him to bleed at every pore. This very real mental and spiritual anguish is what the scriptures refer to as having a 'broken heart and contrite spirit.' (See 3 Nephi 9:20) Such a spirit is the absolute prerequisite for true repentance." (*Ensign*, Oct. 1989, p. 2)

Godly sorrow, then, is an inward awareness that moves transgressors toward the deep desire to cleanse their lives of the stains of transgression. It is a growing consciousness of the gravity and harmful affects of sin and how those sinful choices have hurt not only their souls, but the souls of those with whom they have associated. It becomes the further sensibility of God's sorrow for what has happened—His pain, His grief and His emotions over not only the devastating choices of precious sons or daughters but how those choices have hurt and harmed many innocent souls surrounding them.

Furthermore, godly sorrow entails adopting deep humility and the awareness that the "Holy Messiah. . .offereth himself a sacrifice for sin" only to those who "have a broken heart and contrite spirit." (2ⁿᵈ Nephi 2:6-7) It is the realization that "there is no flesh that can dwell in the presence of God, save it be through the merits, and mercy, and grace of the Holy Messiah." (2ⁿᵈ Nephi 2:8)

The following narrative describes the process of a man who began to experience the kind of godly sorrow that moved him toward true repentance after a prolonged addiction to pornography and other sexual sins. His experience is as follows:

I received a testimony of the church as a teenager. I got reasonable grades, I was an Eagle Scout, and served an honorable full-time mission. When I married (my wife), I was hopelessly in love with her. I wanted everything for her and our new family. We built a life together that included the Lord, church service, graduate school, a career, and several beautiful children.

Although I had exposed myself to pornography since I was a teenager, I never really considered it a part of my life. They were brief exposures that I simply didn't think much of. As the stresses of life started building, I started finding my curiosity for pornography exciting and an escape from the real world. It was a "stay on the diet but check out the menu" mindset that I never really considered adulterous—and certainly didn't consider myself as being untrue to my wife. The fact that I was "staying on the diet" and not actually having sex with someone else seemed to be a safe line to draw. But those escapes started to get more frequent and for a period of two or three years, I found myself blatantly involved in pornography and topless bars. The "safe line" became more and more fuzzy.

During that time, I kept my indiscretions from my wife by lies and deceit but the spirit of darkness was very apparent in my lack of enthusiasm for family and church. I decided to repent and confessed to my bishop. My confession was in a spirit of full disclosure and I determined to live my life differently. However, I chose not to tell (my wife) the full reasons for my life changes—nor was I specific with the bishop. The habits were hard to break but I did it. I became actively engaged in the church and my family again.

(My wife) found joy in the changes and assumed my sins were Word of Wisdom related. I felt love come back into my heart and the Spirit back into my life. I was called to serve in several roles in the church and I felt worthy to serve.

Some time later, I was out of town on a business trip during a particularly stressful time and found myself at a topless bar. When I went home, I knew I needed to confess but for a variety of reasons, I didn't. I rationalized that it was a minor offense because I was "just looking." My rationalization then allowed me to have four more incidents over a four-year period. Each time, I sorely regretted the decision and determined that it would never happen again. After a self-styled repentance, I continued to try and serve faithfully.

My wife and I moved for business reasons but my lack of confession still haunted me. About a year after the move, I found myself in a hotel room viewing pornography in just the way I had determined never to do again. The very next Sunday, I asked for an appointment with my bishop. I decided to repent the Lord's way no matter what the consequences would be.

The bishop counseled me to confess to my wife. I knew that the knowledge of my sins would be hurtful to her and I didn't want to hurt her. I was also afraid that confession would lead to a rejection. Though I rationalized with unselfish motives, I was more selfish than I realized. It took me over two weeks to finally follow the bishop's counsel.

Telling (my wife) was devastating to her. She was crushed. It came as a complete surprise. Her first reactions were supportive but as the realization of what I had done sunk in, her world caved in with it. Hurting her was one of the hardest parts of my repentance. But it was also one of the biggest deterrents in keeping me from sinning again. Eliminating secrecy and deception was the key factor in dispelling the allure of pornography.

As part of my process for repenting, I took an inventory of all of my sins from my past. As that inventory started to unfold, I was surprised with the extent of the incidents. Each time I had an episode I would regret the incident, resolve to never do it again and then put it out of my mind. Having repressed each incident, the details were not always clear and it took me four days of fasting and prayer to come up with a full and complete history that I felt was accurate. As I looked at the timeline I had created, I started to see a recurring pattern that I hadn't really considered; I was caught in an addictive cycle.

(My wife) reviewed the timeline with me and helped me complete it. But it was a painful process. Each new memory of an incident that would arise became a new dagger that cut her to the core. Seeing her agonizing pain made me reluctant to share details. That reluctance would then be interpreted by (my wife) as an attempt to cover up again. But my path had been set. I had determined to repent the Lord's way—which meant being "rigorously honest" with the details. I tried hard to come up with the details that (my wife) asked for, even though it was painful for both of us.

I continued to refine the timeline for a period of about three weeks. We finally reached a point that I felt I had shared everything there was to share. It was hard for me to face the depth to which I had gone. I knew it, but I was afraid to face it. Now, here it was right in front of me in the form of the timeline I had written up. I was disgusted with myself. I wasn't the man people thought I was. I was a fake and a fraud. I saw how I had lied not only to (my wife) but to myself.

I watched (my wife) become disgusted with me and saw her shrivel with her own feelings of rejection and disillusionment. (My wife) began to question whether she could continue to live with a man like me regardless of whether I repented or not. For her, she had completely trusted in my love and in my spiritual counsel. She felt I had become a good father and husband and she had trusted me spiritually. We had a "good" marriage. Now all of that seemed a sham, a hoax, a lie that she believed, hook, line, and sinker. To her, I was playing a cruel game for over twenty years of marriage and she determined that she didn't want anything to do with it anymore. She felt "gypped" because she had put her whole heart and soul into our marriage and family only to find that her "devoted partner" was playing her for a fool. She could no longer trust in her feelings of trust. Her whole world—and how she made sense of it—was turned upside down and it was difficult for her to find things she could believe in. One thing was certain—she couldn't trust me again. She would not allow herself to be vulnerable a second time.

The next eight months proved to be my darkest days. I found myself teetering on the brink of divorce. I was disfellowshipped from the church and felt like I was outcast from the ward. My employment became tentative and there was a question as to whether I would have a job. My children seemed distant and my eldest child seemed especially disgusted with me. I felt worthless, hopeless and completely rejected. Here is an example of one of my journal entries seventy-one days after my disfellowshipment.

Thursday, Day 71:

This was a terrible day. Last night was a terrible night. As I talked with (my wife) she expressed without any malice, complete disgust in me. . . .I didn't sleep much and when I got up I couldn't eat. I was reluctant to take on the day. I have lost hope. I am disgusted with myself. I feel that if I were (my wife), I would leave me. If I were giving (my wife) advice, I would tell her to leave me. I feel a complete sense of loss and hopelessness.

This is no more just a setback that I can fix. It is not a matter of having fallen and I just need to get up again. It isn't that I can't win. It was that I didn't win. I lost. The last game of the last season is over and I lost. I can't fix it. I have failed and there is no way to redeem that failure.

This is not a question of (my wife) forgiving me so that everything would go back to the way it was. Everything that was is now dead. It can never be like it was. It can't be fixed. It is over.

I still feel a determination to see through my repentance. But I can't restore my marriage or my family. My life is over. I ache for what I have lost. I ache for the pain I have caused. I ache to the point of being physically ill. I don't have any sense of what to do next. I feel completely broken. I feel completely lost.

But the Savior never abandoned me. At the moments of complete despair, I would have some ray of hope come into my life that would reassure me and keep me on the path I had chosen. The following journal entry from the next day illustrated how the Savior would come at the darkest moments with a ray of hope:

    Friday, Day 72

        I was feeling pretty lost on the drive into work and I saw a rainbow stretched out over the highway in front of me. It reminded me of a talk that I had heard of the Lord sending a sign of hope to those who are brokenhearted. For a minute I wondered if the rainbow was a sign to me that the Lord was mindful of me. I quickly dismissed the thought, thinking that is not how the Lord speaks to me. (You only hear those types of talks in Relief Society, not Priesthood Meeting.) Of course that beautiful rainbow stretching out so beautifully for everyone to see wouldn't have been there for just one person, especially one as despicable as me.

        Then I had a powerful impression that yes, this was for me! Perhaps the heavens rejoice over my determination to repent. I saw in that rainbow some evidence that I was still loved. I cried in the car. My tears are flowing as I write. I still feel a sense of deep loss and grief. Nevertheless, I believe that the Lord is mindful of me. I am lost but not forgotten.

During that time I went to a counselor and started the process of life change. My counselor helped me keep hope alive by sharing principles and then helping me translate them into behaviors. Counseling helped me identify "drift points" that allow vulnerability to temptations. He also helped me gain a vision of new life patterns that would help me be a better father and husband.

I started to go to work an hour earlier so I could be home earlier. I bowed out of a business opportunity that would have required more of my time. I began participating in more family activities and tried to attend most of my children's extracurricular activities. I also made the effort each week to connect one-on-one with my children. I started attending family events and reunions that I used to avoid and have tried to reach out to our extended family. I started exercising regularly.

Despite my standing, my attendance at church remained uninterrupted. I attended baptisms and priesthood ordinations for family and friends, even though attending always invited the unavoidable questions of my non-participation as a priesthood holder. Although the temptation to isolate myself from the ward seemed the easier course, I tried to stay involved. I continued to pay a full tithe and a generous fast offering without interruption.

I tried to spend more time with my wife. I made an effort to go to bed with her at night. When we discussed the difficult issues between us, I tried to listen and focus on my own actions and choices rather than on hers. I fasted and prayed often for her healing to occur. I wanted to assist her in overcoming the pain she felt.

On the surface nothing seemed to change. I still went to work every day. I still attended church. I still had a daily routine. But inside, everything was changing. It was like a chicken's egg. From the outside, things seemed much the same. But on the inside a new man was being born.

I was lucky to have an inspired bishop who loved me and continued to encourage me on a weekly basis. He had the courage to teach me that I was not as humble as I thought I was and that I was more self-centered than I realized. He pointed out my selfish motives, which I presumed to be altruistic. He shared articles describing the cycle of sin and how to break it. He taught me about having a pure heart that no longer desires sin. I will forever be grateful for the many hours he gave me.

One of the effects of pornography is the desensitization to my own feelings. I was counseled as part of my recovery and repentance to keep a journal, which I did. In the journal, I wrote down my feelings, concerns and the things I was learning. I have come to really appreciate a journal and the self-awareness it has created.

 I have listed some of the lessons I have learned through this:

  Time is an important part in the repentance process. The forging of one's character is always over time. Wisdom comes over time. Education comes over time. Charity comes over time. Testimony comes over time. Each of us is only given a certain amount of time. Once that moment in time is gone, it is lost forever. Perhaps the greatest setback of sin is the time that is misspent that can never be recovered. Our mortal life, our allocated time, is precious. Even when the Savior heals a disease instantly, health comes by living a healthy lifestyle over time. A pure heart must come at a price that is paid over time.

  Self-pity is not humility. Humility is being willing to learn and receive counsel. Humility is recognizing that you don't have all the answers. Humility is willing to do things the Lord's way. Humility is realizing that you need a Savior—not in some theoretical way but because you are lost otherwise. There are some things you can't do for yourself. There are some things you can't fix once they are broken.

 I also learned about love—how unconditional love is the healing agent that can heal both the sinner and the one sinned against. I learned about the gifts of charity and how to strive for them—that one needs to love first and not wait to be loved. The feeling of being loved follows loving others.

 I learned that repentance and forgiveness are linked. Full repentance requires full forgiveness of others. And the process of forgiving is similar to the process of repenting. Asking for forgiveness meant that I had to be willing to forgive.

 I learned about the power of prayer and the atonement of Christ. Silent prayers often helped me avoid my "drift points" and have allowed me to quickly dismiss inappropriate thoughts and feelings. Prayer has guided me during the conflicts with my wife. I have received quiet inspiration during prayer and scripture reading that I keep in my journal and that have guided me throughout my repentance process. I feel that the Savior has become "my" Savior.

I have faced the prospect of losing everything dear to me, including my family. I have watched what I thought was a strong marriage crumble from within, due to my choices, and I have been powerless to fix it. I have watched the woman that I love with all my heart become devastated and disillusioned with me—because of me. I have felt completely helpless and, at times, hopeless and worthless. Yet I have felt guided and directed by my Savior. I am convinced that He brought me to the point of confession. He brought me to the point of confessing to my wife. He helped me reconstruct my history of sin so that I saw how deep I was and how skewed my judgment had been. He has given me a peace and comfort throughout this difficult period but most importantly, He has given me back my conscience.

My overwhelming feelings are feelings of gratitude. I am grateful to be back into the church. I feel that I am right with the Lord. It is not that I feel my repentance process is done. I am still more self-centered than I should be. I am not as humble as I should be. I don't listen as much as I should and I need more patience. But I have done things the Lord's way and in that sense, I feel right with the Lord.

I am still married and although progress seems slow, we are progressing. I have learned that time can be ordained for my good if used wisely. My relationships with my children are improving. My work life is getting better. I am no longer hiding anything. There is still much repenting that I have to do, but I feel the Lord has purged the desire for sexual sin from my heart. I feel grateful. I have felt a miracle in my life.

Looking back is paradoxical to me. I would give anything to have not sinned in the first place. So much time and so much of life has passed me by. I have hurt my wife so deeply and scarred my family in so many ways that I deeply regret. It is hard to take responsibility for hurting people you love.

At the same time, I am grateful for what I have learned about myself and about the Savior. I am grateful for what I have learned about love, patience, and humility. I have learned how to rely on my Savior because "I can't fix it." An enormous sense of gratitude is born from being completely broken and forgotten and then "redeemed." Without my experience, would I have ever felt as broken or lost? Would I have ever felt as grateful if I hadn't felt so undesirable? I have a testimony of the tender mercies of the Savior. I am grateful for the miracle in my life.

As shown from the example above, the Savior truly can take those lost in sin and lead them toward a life of wholeness when they experience godly sorrow and then allow His healing hand to come into their lives. A sobering reality often exists for many of these transgressors. Often they have fallen victim to darkness without having the faintest idea that their choices would so adversely affect the innocent souls surrounding them in such deep and devastating ways. This can be illustrated symbolically in the following true account. The story is told of George A. Smith, the "potato saint" for whom St. George is named, and how in his family's time of great hunger and need, he would peel off the skins of the potatoes for himself to eat and leave the rest—the bulk of the potato—to his starving family. Little did he realize that the act of taking out the nutrients in the skins would eventually save him but it resulted in his family's failed health. He so grieved over his choices that he later left crops of potatoes for others thus starving.

How representative this could be of those who have participated in sexual sin without realizing how deeply it would hurt those innocent souls surrounding them. As more and more light comes into their lives, they often are moved to mourn over what they have done that has caused so much damage and destruction to innocent parties surrounding them. Philip A. Harrison, in his book *Clean Hands, Pure Heart*, gives an example that illustrates this. He said,

As I began my amends list, my heart ached because I immediately thought of my dear wife, Kathy. We were married for almost 29 years before she died from heart disease. She lived with me through most of my years of addiction, and even though I hid it from her, and I think she was genuinely happy most of the time, but I had to admit I could have been a far better husband to her if I had not been enslaved to lust. How many times was I not there for her emotionally, physically, spiritually, and even sexually because I was focused on my addiction? How many hours did I steal from her to feed my habit? How many lies did I tell her in order to hide my actions? There are so many things for which I want to ask her forgiveness. Furthermore, in addition to the actions that hurt her as a direct result of my addiction, I have to acknowledge she was hurt by my other faults as well.

I always thought of myself as a good husband, but now I know I could have been more unselfish and more thoughtful. I could have made life better for my wife than I did. I don't say this to needlessly dump guilt on myself, but rather to honestly inventory my relationships and see where repair was needed.

. . .The next people on my amends list were my children. I had to face the hard questions concerning them: How *have* I harmed my children? Was I ever too severe in physically punishing them? How many times was I unavailable to them? How many opportunities to be with and enjoy them did I miss? And what about the missed teaching opportunities? How many times did I not bear my testimony to them, because I didn't feel the Spirit in my own life at the moment? How many principles did I not teach them because doing so made me feel like a hypocrite? And how many times did I blame them or put them on the defensive to hide my own sins?

. . .I still wonder how much my failings have contributed to problems my children have had or will yet have in their lives. (pp. 171-172)

With the Savior's help and sustaining strength, transgressors can become aware of the wounds they have inflicted but then move on from those to become instruments of healing to those they once hurt and scarred by their choices.

"Inasmuch as Ye Have Humbled Yourselves Before Me, the Blessings of the Kingdom are Yours" (D&C 61:37)

Sometimes, despite the fact that transgressors do feel godly sorrow and are trying to sincerely repent, they often feel judged and thwarted by others who do not acknowledge their changes of heart or the reformation of their behaviors. As they continue forward on their paths of repentance, their fruits and consistent actions will pave the way for renewed hope and trust. Richard G. Scott had this to say regarding transgressors in these circumstances:

> If loved ones seem to ignore you, it is because they don't know what to do. Their past attempts to help have been rejected; you have not wanted help. Reach out to them trustingly. Ask for support in your sincere efforts to change. Give them reason to know that this time is different because you will do it the Lord's way.
>
> As you make progress on the way back, you will discover feelings that you haven't had for a long time—feelings of concern for others, feelings of unselfish love, feelings of a desire to be near loved ones, and of self-respect and confidence. These stirrings are evidence of progress, like a growing light at the end of a tunnel.
>
> . . .I promise you, in the name of the Lord, that He will help you. He will be there in every time of need. He gave His life so that you can change your life. I promise you that you'll feel His love, strength and support. Trust Him completely. He is not going to make any mistakes. He knows what He is doing. (*Ensign*, May 0, pp. 75-76).

7

"Satan Seeketh to Turn Their Hearts Away From the Truth, That They Become Blinded" (D&C 78:10)

Another necessary tool needed to heal from the extensive damage of sexual sin is to discern and overcome Satan's tactics and schemes—his lies and deceptions—used to entrap transgressors. It is through our Savior and His power that Satan can be overcome in this way, for "whosoever will may lay hold upon the word of God. . .which shall divide asunder all the cunning and the snares and the wiles of the devil, and lead the man of Christ in a strait and narrow course across that everlasting gulf of misery which is prepared to engulf the wicked." (Helaman 3:29)

Satan truly is a cunning and experienced general that has used his forces throughout eons to wage an evil, bitter warfare—warfare meant to destroy the souls of men so that they suffer "a death, even a second death, which is a spiritual death" and "die as to things pertaining unto righteousness." (Alma 40:26) He overcame many souls before this mortal life and he continues to win souls during this existence. One of Satan's greatest tools and weapons today is sexual sin—sin that ensnares and leaves behind immense devastation.

The adversary has slyly made sexual sin seem enticing, beautiful and freeing, but it is entrapping, venomous, and highly addictive. It pollutes and darkens those souls who have participated in it, sometimes completely obliterating the power of free will and choice. It hurts and harms the innocent souls surrounding them. The evil spirits assigned to this plague are powerful, cunning and skillful, working relentlessly to defeat and destroy. They make evil appear exciting and attractive, tempting men and women to partake of it seemingly without consequence. Their voices are alluring and seductive. They call "evil good and good evil" and "put darkness for light, and light for darkness." (2nd Nephi 15:20)

"Who has not heard and felt the enticings of the devil?" James E. Faust has asked. "His voice often sounds so reasonable and his message so easy to justify. It is an enticing, intriguing voice with dulcet tones. It is neither hard nor discordant. No one would listen to Satan's voice if it sounded harsh or mean. If the devil's voice were unpleasant, it would not entice people to listen to it."

James E. Faust then warns, "(Satan) is working under such perfect disguise that many do not recognize either him or his methods." But, he adds, "There is no crime he would not commit, no debauchery he would not set up, no plague he would not send, no heart he would not break, no life he would not take, no soul he would not destroy. He comes as a thief in the night; he is a wolf in sheep's clothing." (*Ensign,* Nov. 1987, p. 34) As Dallin H. Oaks stated, "What the devil portrays as fun can be spiritually fatal." (*Ensign,* Nov. 2004, p. 45) Satan comes to defeat and destroy our Father's precious sons and daughters and has succeeded in many cases by getting them to participate in sexual sin.

Satan's growing power and control over the people of the world because of sexual sin could be compared to the enemy forces that overtook many parts of Europe during World War II. Those forces were dark, ruthless and merciless. They killed and destroyed any who got in their way. Their intent was to entrap, enslave and overpower, taking away all freedoms. Many innocent souls became trapped under this dark regime and suffered intensely. There was anguish, pain, grief, devastation and suffering left in the wake of this overpowering enemy. There were many made to

> . . .bow down with grief, sorrow, and care, under the most damning hand of murder, tyranny, and oppression, supported and urged on and upheld by the influence of that spirit which hath so strongly riveted the creeds of the fathers, who have inherited lies, upon the hearts of the children, and filled the world with confusion, and has been growing stronger and stronger, and is now the very mainspring of all corruption, and the whole earth groans under the weight of its iniquity.
>
> It is an iron yoke, it is a strong band; they are the very handcuffs, and chains, and shackles, and fetters of hell. (D&C 123:7-8)

The Lord, in His great wisdom and mercy, has been preparing His forces for "D-day"—His great counter-offensive against Satan's onslaughts and the darkness that has been brought in through sexual sin. The Lord desires to free many of His choice sons and daughters from His eternal enemy's hold on them. He has prepared generals—prophets and other spiritual leaders—who have carefully studied Satan's tactics of warfare and who speak openly and strongly against the ramifications of sexual sin. He has prepared battalions of righteous men and women whose intent is to help those trapped by darkness—both transgressors and those who have been hurt by them—and free them from bondage. Battalions include experienced bishops and Stake Presidents; support groups—both within and without the Church; men of God who are well-trained counselors and therapists; and even the support of others who have been trapped by sexual sin but are now freed and are "a spokesman unto this people." (D&C 100:9) Books on the subject of sexual sin are increasing and act like bombs against the enemy, too, weakening their strongholds. Truly, the Lord is doing all within his power to help His beloved sons and daughters escape the devastation of sexual sin and become healed and whole once more.

Part of the freedom from sexual sin comes from discerning

the tactics Satan has used and overcoming them so that "Satan may have no more power upon the hearts of the children of men." (Ether 8:25) As the Lord has admonished, "Pray always, that you may come off conqueror; yea, that you may conquer Satan, and that you may escape the hands of the servants of Satan that do uphold his work." (D&C 10:5) Some of Satan's greatest lies and deceptions are as follows:

"There's nothing wrong with having sexual desires. It's natural and a part of life. Everyone has those desires, and everyone pursues gratification of them. So can I—in whatever ways I want." Some of Satan's greatest grips around transgressors come from these subtle ideas which can eventually lead someone from just toying with sexual desire to ultimate bondage and entrapment in addictive sin. President James E. Faust once said, "Some of Satan's most appealing lines are 'Everyone does it'; 'If it doesn't hurt anybody else, it's all right'; 'If you feel all right about it, it's OK'; or 'it's the "in" thing to do.' These subtle entreaties make Satan the great imitator, the master deceiver, the arch counterfeiter, and the great forger." (Ibid., p. 34).

In relation to pornography, for example, Satan might say, "A little bit won't hurt; I can always just look once, participate once, engage it in just once—and then walk away. Everyone has these same desires and everyone does it. Besides, it only affects me. This has nothing to do with anyone or anything around me. I'm the only one who needs to worry about this or suffer the consequences of this." Even one participation in pornography, however, can stimulate physical reactions and emotions that engender addiction—and that can become a raging wildfire that burns completely out of control, destroying everything and everyone around it. Participation, too, brings in the loss of the Spirit and the resulting darkness from Satan's influence—another factor that can lead to bondage.

As another example, a woman and a man who have become emotionally involved outside the bonds of marriage may adopt such reasoning as, "Hugging and kissing, to express affection as friends, is totally acceptable. I would express affection like this to anyone I liked and appreciated. It's okay that we become physically involved in this way." Small rationalizations such as these have many times led to adulterous relationships which have destroyed eternal covenants and marriages completely.

Truly it is the small steps, the subtle rationalizations pertaining to sexual sin, which Satan uses to lead someone to ultimate enslavement. James E. Faust quoted C. S. Lewis when he said, "It does not matter how small the sins are, provided that their cumulative effect is to edge the man away from the light and out into the Nothing. . .Indeed, the safest road to Hell is the gradual one—the gentle slope, soft underfoot, without sudden turnings, without milestones, without signposts. (*The Screwtape Letters, p. 56)" (Ensign,* Nov. 1987, p. 35)

"Keep sexual sin in the dark; it is my private concern and no one else's. If I've confessed my mistakes to my bishop, no one else needs to know. It's my personal problem." There are many that "seek deep to hide their counsel from the Lord! And their works are in the dark." (2nd Nephi 27:27) Satan and his forces truly love the dark. They love secrecy, hiding and concealment. Their greatest chains are forged in darkness as they convince transgressors that their sins are minor, that they're unknown and therefore not hurting anyone, that "perhaps I did make a mistake, but I won't do it again—so everything is okay. I'll just keep this between me and the Lord. No one else needs to know." This reasoning soothes consciences until the next time of participation, when the patterns of darkness and secrecy are repeated—sometimes over and over and over again until thick chains of addiction are formed.

In order to break the bonds of sexual sin, sins must be brought into the light. As the scriptures state, "The Lord God worketh not in darkness." (2nd Nephi 26:23) Part of coming into the Lord's light is full and complete confession—taking sins out of Satan's web of secrecy and exposing them to the light of Christ. A bishop or Stake President should hear a complete confession, but also those who have made sacred covenants with transgressors should, as well. As it has been stated in *Heal My Broken Heart,*

. . .the wives of a transgressor *must* become a part of. . .confession. The reasoning for confessing to a wife is twofold. First of all, when a marriage occurs, a covenant relationship is made in a triangular pattern between the Savior, the husband and the wife. When the covenant relationship is broken between the wife and the husband because of transgression, the wife has the right and indeed must know the transgression *in this life* in order to heal this broken covenant relationship.

. . .Confession of sins to both the wife and the appropriate priesthood holders is an essential part of purging. If those sins are confessed and healed in this life, then, as the Lord has said, "He who has repented of his sins, the same is forgiven, and I, the Lord, *remember them no more*. By this ye may know if a man repenteth of his sins—behold, he will *confess them* and forsake them." (D&C 58:42-43, italics added)

There is a second reason a transgressor should confess to a wife. As one bishop said, when a transgressor only confesses to the priesthood authority over him and not to his partner, this is like two men "colluding" against the wife. It is unfair and unjust to the one truly injured and betrayed by the sin. It is not only the covenant with the Savior that has been broken by the transgression, but also the covenant with the wife. She has a right and a responsibility to know when this has happened.

Serious spiritual danger also results from not confessing to a wife. The transgressor often feels safe from accountability. This opens him up to incomplete healing and the possibility of future sin. What does he have to lose if he sins again when his wife will always be unaware of what is happening? Is there any risk involved if his partner never knows his actions?

Unless there is complete, total confession to the proper priesthood authorities and a wife, true healing *will not* follow. . . .

As the Prophet Joseph Smith has said, "Let. . .all the Saints be willing to confess all their sins, and not keep back a part." (*Teachings*, p. 155) (Davidson/Davies, pp. 32-34)

When there is not a full and complete confession, almost inevitably a transgressor will sin again. As Sheri Dew stated in her book *No One Can Take Your Place*, "Unrepented sin makes us vulnerable to more sin. . . .When you hide a sin, or lie about a sin, it seems to almost guarantee that at some point—an hour later, a day later, a week later, ten years later—you will repeat the sin. . . .The only thing that breaks the cycle is confession and repentance." (p. 108)

"Secrecy and the Hiding of Sin Resulted from my Deep Love and Concern for Others, not from Deception." Satan keeps many trapped in darkness by convincing them to believe that secrecy and deception are needed so as to not hurt those they love—that they're doing others favors by keeping darkness hidden. This clever trap of the adversary is designed to soothe consciences by convincing transgressors it is true love and concern that allows them to continue as they are. They don't want to hurt their partners or others; they don't want to create wounds in the innocent. Why would they do something that would hurt those they care about by exposing secrets that would do just that?

This sly thinking can be counteracted by the simple idea that true love and caring would be characterized by complete fidelity and unbroken trust. It does not encompass lies, deception and betrayal. Most transgressors become convinced that they were being noble in not sharing their misdeeds as efforts to shield those they love. Until they see this pattern of thinking for the lie that it is, they will often continue it—even during attempts at "confession." It is not nobility but selfishness and self-concern that are the basis of this type of reasoning.

"If it's between a husband and wife, it's okay." Another cunning trap of Satan is the reasoning that anything which occurs between a husband and wife in a marital relationship is okay and justified. Often this type of thinking has excused behaviors that are a result of sexual sin. For example, one woman stated she had participated in intimacy "that would almost want to make me throw up" until she realized her husband had been involved in deep sexual sin, transgressions which he had carefully hidden from her.

Sometimes this type of thinking—"it's okay between a husband and wife"—also allows behaviors that can ultimately lead to sexual sin. For example, there have been wives who have agreed to watch pornographic materials with their husbands under the guise that "it will stimulate more chemistry between us" and "it's okay if you and I are looking at it together." The harm done to both parties is real and lasting, however, even if they do participate together. Often a husband moves on to more intense sexual drives and addictions. Many times a woman feels like nothing more than property or chattel used for selfishness—not as a partner or someone loved and cherished. Spouses usually feel their partners' straying hearts and emotional distance more and more and they may be confused as to why it is happening—especially when they were so willing to try and please or accommodate them. Furthermore, there are more and more women developing sexual addictions that are becoming binding, as well. Sexual sin, in whatever form, damages and destroys good relationships and the foundation for true and lasting intimacy.

"I did these things to better enrich mine and my wife's intimacy. I was thinking of my wife when I did them." These cunning lies of Satan are a means of justification for sexual sin, particularly where pornography is involved. Transgressors have often justified participation by claiming, "I was doing this to enhance the physical intimacy between me and my spouse. I wanted to learn things that would please my wife and make me a better lover. I was doing it for her." Another cunning idea is "I was thinking of my wife when I was looking at the other person, thinking of her and not that person." These subtle lies can easily be discerned for the falsehoods they are, but they are a common justification for participation in lust and emotional adultery—a sin just as damaging as actual physical adultery. The Lord made no distinction between the actual physical act or the act of emotional

adultery when he said, "He that looketh on a woman to lust after her, or if any shall commit adultery in their hearts, they shall not have the Spirit, but shall deny the faith and shall fear." (D&C 63:16) He then warns that if that person "repents not" of these things "he shall be cast out." (D&C 42:23)

"My partner's lacks and dysfunction caused my sins; the resulting problems in our marriage lie with my partner, as well." This type of reasoning is one of Satan's most powerful tools in leading transgressors away from marriages and sacred eternal covenants. He convinces transgressors that the problems—the darkness, contention, unrest, imbalance, agitation or discord they feel—lie from sources outside of them and have been created by others, not by themselves or their wicked choices. Satan often convinces them they must leave or get out of relationships so they won't have to deal with the negative emotions they feel. However, as Alma counseled his son Corianton, "Do not endeavor to excuse yourself in the least point because of your sins, by denying the justice of God; but do you let the justice of God, and his mercy, and his long-suffering have full sway in your heart; and let it bring you down to the dust in humility." (Alma 42:30)

Another cunning trap is to convince transgressors that if marital problems do exist, the fault lies with their partners and their partners' reactions, not with themselves or the devastation they have created. This reasoning is often used even if transgressors are trying to repent. For example, when one woman tried to express to her husband how his sexual sins devastated her because she had "loved him so deeply and given him a pure offering as a wife in the past," he turned on her and said, "If you had truly loved me, then you wouldn't be feeling the way you do now. You would be patient and long-suffering with me and not blame me as you have done. You don't have the pure love of Christ because true love—charity—would cause you to have reacted differently and to have treated me differently than you do. There wouldn't be these issues between us if you loved me as you claim to have loved me." Similar types of reasoning are often used by the adversary to have transgressors shift blame and responsibility to others outside them instead of taking responsibility for their grievous choices and actions.

"Partaking of the 'forbidden fruit'—participating in forbidden sexual sin—will help me more than harm me." Satan is a master manipulator. He not only creates problems that leave gaping holes in the sons and daughters of God, but then he gives his solutions to solving those problems he's created—solutions that hurt and harm further. As with Adam and Eve, Satan makes people feel uncomfortable with their situations, their standing and status—"Ye shall not eat of every tree of the garden?" (Moses 4:4)—and then he presents solutions that will only hurt and harm further.

Such it is with those who participate in sexual sin. Often Satan has created many of the problems in transgressors' homes and lives, and then he presents solutions to those problems—partaking of the "forbidden fruit"—to solve those problems. For example, Satan convinces many men who suffer from low self-esteem and lack of self-confidence that pornography will bring them the gratification and pleasure they need to feel good about themselves. For others, he may convince them that such and such a person outside of the marriage relationship will bring happiness and fulfillment, not current spouses or marriages.

Adopting Satan's solutions to problems is similar to standing in quicksand and Satan tosses a rope as a means of escape—only to pull that person deeper into the sand and ensnare them further. Satan truly creates problems and issues and then gives damaging solutions to those problems. It is his intent to "deceive and blind men, and to lead them captive at his will, even as many as w(ill) not hearken unto (the Lord's) voice." (Moses 4:4) Adopting the Lord's solutions to wholeness and happiness—not the adversary's—is the only safe escape route.

"I'm not sure I believe in God anymore." Another cunning snare of Satan is to have someone change core beliefs so that sins can be justified. When people engage in sin and dissonance is created inside their hearts and spirits, they have two choices. They can either repent and forsake their sins—thus creating harmony

once again—or they can nullify the whisperings of conscience by changing internal beliefs or realities. Many transgressors lose their faith in our Heavenly Father and the Savior because by so doing they can rationalize the breaking of commandments and sacred covenants made before them. Others often create new realities based on lies and become so "possessed with a lying spirit" (Alma 30:42) that they "verily believe" that those lies are "true." (Alma 30:53) For example, one woman claimed she had "always been so thwarted, discouraged and depressed" around her husband that she had to get out of that bondage by participating in adultery with another man. Another man claimed his wife was so ultra religious and fanatical in her views about God that her warped and twisted thinking regarding religion had becoming damaging to him, thus making him have to leave the marriage to maintain his own spiritual and mental wholeness. He soon after entered into a marriage relationship with another woman.

Richard G. Scott has said, "Satan would have you rationalize—that is, twist something you know to be true into a pattern that appears to support your deviation from truth. Rationalization leads you down blind alleys in life. It drains spiritual power. It barricades the path to happiness because it distorts your understanding of truth." (*Ensign,* May 1990, p. 76) Rationalization and changing truth is one of Satan's greatest tools used to justify sins and lead someone to bondage.

"I have done the 'Five R's' of repentance—therefore, I've overcome my sins. Others outside of me are the problems if there are problems that still exist. Their lack of forgiveness is worse than my sins, anyway, so the problems lie with them—not with me." There is a huge difference between intellectual humility and true humility. Intellectual humility—thinking of one's own self as humble and repentant—is so very different than humbling a soul deeply and sincerely before God. The humble, repentant person cares about being right before God more than anything else—more than reputation, outside opinions or social standing. The truly humble person also cares about others and the damage done to them instead of blaming, criticizing, finding fault or condemning

them for choices and actions. True repentance engenders patience, love, caring, forgiveness and selfless service. It does not produce ceaseless judgment and criticism, causing one to endlessly point out weaknesses and faults in others.

Intellectual humility is another form of pride—pride paraded under the guise of meekness. President Ezra Taft Benson described this kind of pride when he said, "The central feature of pride is enmity—enmity toward God and enmity toward our fellowmen. . . .Selfishness is one of the more common faces of pride. 'How everything affects me' is the center of all that matters—self-conceit, self-pity, worldly self-fulfillment, self-gratification, and self-seeking." He continues, "Pride is the universal sin, the great vice. . .The antidote for pride is humility—meekness, submissiveness. It is the broken heart and the contrite spirit." (*Ensign*, May 1989, p. 4)

When transgressors turn from the "self" part of pride—the selfishness and self-concern—to care for others outside themselves, when they truly become more concerned with others than with themselves—that is when true repentance and true humility have occurred. This is not the supposed humility from solely overcoming sin and from believing others should see and accept that—and where they are at—as a matter of course. It is deep and lasting humility that changes lives and then brings about efforts toward healing others who have been hurt by their transgressions.

"There's really no hope for me now. I knew I was doing wrong when I sinned, but I still did it anyway. That makes it tantamount to denying the Holy Ghost—the unpardonable sin. Why try to change when it won't make a difference in my life? I've tried to repent before and it doesn't help. I keep going back to my sins. All is lost and I'll never change." These types of thoughts are other common traps used by Satan to keep transgressors in the grips of sin—to make them feel as if they've gone too far to repent and be forgiven. Elder Richard G. Scott has said in relation to this:

Lucifer will do all in his power to keep you

captive. You are familiar with his strategy. He whispers: "No one will ever know." "Just one more time." "You can't change; you have tried before and failed." "It's too late; you've gone too far." Don't let him discourage you.

. . .Freedom from your transgression will come through sincere faith, true repentance, willing obedience, and the giving of self.

. . .Don't live your life in despair, feeling sorry for yourself because of the mistakes you have made. Let the sunshine in by doing the right things—now. (*Ensign,* May 1990, pp. 74-75)

Boyd K. Packer had this to say regarding repentance and forgiveness:

The gospel teaches us that relief from torment and guilt can be earned through repentance. Save for those few who defect to perdition after having known a fullness, there is no habit, no addiction, no rebellion, no transgression, no offense exempted from the promise of complete forgiveness. . ."There is never a time," the Prophet Joseph Smith taught, "when the spirit is too old to approach God. *All are within the reach of pardoning mercy, who have not committed the unpardonable sin.*"

. . .I bear witness of Christ and of the power of His atonement. And I know that "his anger kindleth against the wicked; they repent, and in a moment it is turned away, and they are in his favor, and he giveth them life; therefore, weeping may endure for a night, but joy cometh in the morning." (JST, Ps. 30:5) (*Ensign,* Nov. 1995, p. 19- 21, italics added)

As illustrated by the examples above, there are countless ways and means that Satan can deceive and destroy through his cunning and wiles. The Lord promises, however, to help deliver those who turn to Him from the enslaving traps of Satan and his powerful forces. It is through our Savior that He will give those "faithful. . .the victory" (D&C 104:82). The Lord has promised, "He that endureth in faith and doeth my will, the same *shall overcome*." (D&C 63:20, italics added)

8

"I Would Speak Unto You that Are Pure in Heart" (Jacob 3:2)

Not only does Satan deceive, beguile and harm transgressors who have sinned, but he works relentlessly on those surrounding transgressors—innocent souls who have been hurt or betrayed by them. These innocent souls include family members, spouses or other associates with whom the transgressors have special ties. So often wounds and attacks have occurred on these innocent souls without their even realizing where those attacks have come from— that they're living with the repercussions of darkness brought in through transgressors' grievous choices. They can often live for years under this kind of darkness without being aware of it and suffer from the internal misery these attacks bring.

Satan desires to trap all through sin and transgression. If he cannot, however—if he knows those souls will not follow darkness in this way, through sin—he cunningly uses different approaches to entrap and ensnare. Satan brings darkness into their lives through such things as discouragement, despair and hopelessness. He often makes these innocent souls feel as if they are less than who they are—that they are not valued, loved or that they will never live up to being someone special in the sight of God. They may feel ugly, overweight, socially inept or backward — inferior in many ways to others surrounding them.

Satan may bring in oppression and discouragement through his dark spirits that can result in heavy depression or mental and emotional illnesses. Sometimes this oppression manifests itself in anxiety, panic attacks or feelings of being completely out of control over the events and circumstances in one's life. Many often feel ceaseless worthlessness and unending inferiority — as a parent, a partner — a husband or wife, as a member of the church, as a friend, as a son or daughter, and so on. Many feel their offerings are not sufficient in their lives and that they will never live up to what they should or ought to be. They in essence feel unaccomplished and insignificant — that their lives do not matter because they do so little, matter so little and offer so little to others.

Other victims often feel devalued, unworthy and of no consequence to God, especially if they've made mistakes in the past. They may feel that no matter what they do, their efforts and offerings will not be acceptable in the sight of the Lord because of who and what they are. They feel the darkness of past mistakes hang over their heads constantly, reminding them of how unworthy they are.

Satan attacks others by making them feel their only value lies in what they have outwardly — physical beauty, a trim figure, a nice and organized house or financial wealth — and if they don't have those, they have no intrinsic worth. Inside they carry deep feelings of insecurity and fear that they will be rejected if they do not retain these outside accomplishments. As long as they are "tan and skinny," though, they are fine. But if these things are taken away, there is panic and a deep fear of rejection and abandonment.

As shown, Satan attacks innocent souls in countless ways, making them feel less than who and what they are. He whispers such things as, "You're an awful parent. You don't spend as much time with your children as you should. You got too angry yesterday and yelled at them; you inflicted harm on them because you're such a terrible person." Or, "You're so ugly and fat. You're not beautiful enough and you never will be. You shouldn't even go out in social situations." Or, "God doesn't love you in any special way. You're one of His countless children. Yes, He loves you, but no differently than He loves billions of others. You are insignificant in His eyes, not loved, valued and cherished as a unique individual He cares for infinitely." Or, "You have made mistakes—think of all you've done wrong. You'll never be able to leave the past behind you; you are an awful, bad person and don't try to hide it under the guise of spirituality. Your choices will always be a part of you and you'll never become a clean and pure child of God." Or Satan may whisper, "The darkness you feel will never change. You've felt this way from day one—depressed, hopeless and despairing—that never-ending discouragement you can't shake. There's no hope for you. Your life will always be this way—dark and oppressive. There's nothing you can do about it. Prayers don't help; scripture reading hasn't made a dent. Your spiritual attempts have never been sufficient or helpful. You might as well give up trying; nothing will ever change. Your life will always be bleak. You'll never feel any light or hope." Satan's attacks are different for each person, but they are real. They can be overpowering and they inevitably damage souls if his whisperings are adopted as truth.

So often what adds depth and severity to these inward attacks is often they are spoken outwardly—through transgressors' voices or accusations. When transgressors become an instrument of Satan—after having bought into his deceptions and cunning through sexual sin—they can then become a tool to afflict and torment in this way. They are many times given what to say to hurt and damage innocent people around them, often hitting on inward weaknesses, vulnerabilities and insecurities. For example, one man would claim his wife was too fat, that she didn't keep a clean, well-running house and that she never understood him—or herself, for that matter. All of these reflected inward weaknesses and insecurities that she had struggled with in her own mind. Her husband constantly criticized her in these ways, showing much impatience and irritation for these supposed lacks.

Transgressors often criticize, condemn, demean and are

impatient with defects similar to this, pointing out those defects whenever there are confrontations, arguments or misunderstandings. They often blame others for inadequacies, faults and imperfections—as if those are the glaring personality traits that exist in them, not the good redeeming qualities they have or the righteous things they've done and accomplished. In other words, transgressors become tools to point out negative behaviors and attributes and rarely acknowledge anything worthwhile, positive or uplifting. They hurt, defeat and damage, not uplift, sustain and help.

Often there exists the feeling that others will never live up to expectations of transgressors—that they'll always live in the darkness of transgressors' disapproval or disapprobation. Transgressors often degrade and devalue contributions and efforts—even those worthy of approval and recognition.

In many cases, even if transgressors are not openly vocal against those around them, they are often withdrawn, uncaring, apathetic and neglectful, not taking time to cultivate relationships—thus giving the silent message that their spouses or others are not valued. These non-verbal communications are as real and damaging as the other direct verbal messages that come. They may cause someone to believe, "I am not valued as a person, a partner, a son or daughter. I am not cared for, loved, treasured or cherished enough to be worthy of time and attention. My offerings as a person are not sufficient or I would be treated differently. I do not matter in this relationship—enough to be remembered, treated correctly or treasured."

Laurie Hall in her book, *An Affair of the Mind,* described this type of neglect in a series of unsent letters she wrote to her husband as a "journal" during a marital separation because of his infidelity. In two of the letters, she writes:

> Dear Jack,
>   I put away the last of the Christmas things today. Oh, how it hurt! . . .Christmas is about family and dreams of family. Putting everything away meant

all the years of longing for a family that was whole were over. Saying Christmas was over meant all my dreams of our life together were as dead as the needles that fell to the carpet under our tree.

Maybe it's part of accepting what is true instead of what I so desperately want to be true. Christmas was always a difficult time for me because you never gave me anything. I know, now, your inability to give was a natural outgrowth of your addiction to pornography. Lust is selfish. It gives nothing unless it can use that gift to get what it wants from the receiver. You were always wondering, "What's in it for me?"

Your lack of effort to get me a gift was always a bit awkward to explain to the kids. They were great tree inspectors, crawling in and out among the gifts, shaking, poking, guessing what might be there. They would always notice there was nothing for me.

"Mommy, how come there isn't anything under the tree for you?"

"When's Daddy going to take us shopping so we can get something for you?"

"I don't need anything. I have you and you're the best gift I could ever get," I'd say and give them a hug.

It doesn't matter, I'd think, because it was true—the children were the best gift I had.

But having my stocking hang empty when everyone else's was bulging on Christmas morning was somehow harder than not having anything under the tree, because you know tree gifts are from people, but we pretend the stocking is from Santa, who knows if you've been naughty or nice. And so I'd choke down the lump of coal in my throat and force back the tears. I must have been very naughty to never get anything.

As they got older, the kids caught on that Santa didn't visit Mommy. So, on Christmas morning, they'd jump up and down shouting, "Check your stock, Mommy, check your stock!" And so I'd take the emaciated thing down from the mantle and I'd find a stick of gum, a pretty picture, a smooth rock, or one of their treasures.

How can you be sad about this? The children love you. It doesn't matter if Jack doesn't, I'd think.

And I lived quite successfully that way for a number of years, until one Christmas morning, I looked at that pathetic stocking and said, "It does matter, and it hurts."

* * *

Dear Jack,

I got the Monitor heater installed today. I wanted the house warm for the kids. I wanted them to know that life is better than living for five years in northern Vermont without heat. I can't figure out why you never put it in. It was here, ready to go. How could you let us be so cold?

It's so hard to get people to understand that your addiction to pornography has broader implications than just having you zoned out over Miss September. Lust made you selfish. You only took care of yourself. You wouldn't take care of us. Lust made you angry. When I'd decided the children had waited long enough to be warm, and I suggested getting someone to install the heater, you got furious and told me you were going to take care of it.

In hindsight, I can see I was the stupid one not to go ahead and risk your anger and put the thing in anyway, but I was trying to hard not to usurp your place of leadership. The people at church told me if I would just trust you, you would rise to the occasion. They didn't understand how I'd been trusting you for years and years. They told me I would be controlling if I took over things that were your responsibility. So, our children were cold for no reason for five long years. I wonder if any of those church folk's children have been cold for no reason.

. . .I feel like an ashamed, forsaken, heartsick, rejected wife. (pp.54-58)

As shown, there are many ways transgressors hurt the innocent souls surrounding them. Transgressors truly become tools in the adversary's hands to afflict extensive damage on those around them. Satan and those transgressors who follow him would drive wedges into others' small weaknesses and imperfections and make them seem unconquerable—as if those weaknesses define who and what they are. Those thus attacked many times feel unworthy, worthless and unloved.

The Lord yearns deeply for His special sons and daughters who have been trapped in this kind of darkness to see the truth of what has happened to them in their lives. In reality, they are beautiful roses with perhaps one or two crushed petals, petals which represent the imperfections and weaknesses that all people have. The darkness surrounding them has caused those souls to concentrate on the miniscule imperfections—those two crushed petals—to make them appear glaring and conspicuous. In truth, the weaknesses are small and do not detract at all from the overall creation they have become—a beautiful flower that has imparted much good, strength and beauty to others.

Righteous women—and faithful men—are one of the most powerful forces under heaven. It is no wonder Satan would attack them to try and weaken them, attempting to take away their real, long and lasting influence—an influence that can permeate generations. Righteousness and faithfulness is the greatest threat to his kingdom on this earth, and Satan spends the majority of his time attacking those who could harm him the most.

The Savior is the key to pushing away Satan's heavy darkness and oppression. He truly has "overcome the world" (D&C 50:41) and all things in it. He can help those in the world overcome their temporal afflictions and trials, as well—no matter how acute, painful, destructive or damaging they've been. It is His eternal calling and mission to do so, and He promises "to open their eyes, and to turn them from darkness to light, and from the power of Satan unto God." (Acts 26:18)

When the Savior's light, love and understanding can reach deeply into hearts and shine through—even amidst the continuing storms of burdens and trials—souls can become healed, whole, assured, calm and happy in Him. There will come rekindled illumination into their spirits as He strengthens, comforts, uplifts, sustains and "speak(s) peace to (their) souls," (Alma 58:11) bringing them that "peace of God that passeth all understanding." (Philippians 4:7)

Like those Jaredites who had to cross the "raging deep" (Ether 3:3) and suffer many days of trial and uncertainty, the Lord will give "light in (their) vessels." (Ether 2:23) He will let them know of His infinite love and caring—that He has shed many tears over their pains, burdens, trials and heartaches. Those wounded can come to drink deeply of this "fountain of living waters" (2nd Nephi 2:25) and find the comfort, peace and perfect love that comes from our Savior in never-ending abundance. Those who do so will come to learn and know Him in a way they never have before. They will discover that they can turn to Him in every experience of their lives for understanding, direction, strength, love, peace, comfort, hope and shelter.

The Savior would surely say to someone thus suffering, "My son (or daughter), peace be unto thy soul; thine adversity and thine afflictions shall be but a small moment; and then, if thou endure it well, God shall exalt thee on high; thou shalt triumph over all thy foes." (D&C 121:6-7)

The Savior would surely say, "My precious daughter or son, do you know it was not my will that this terrible, dark thing happened to you? The unrighteous choices of another caused this hurt and pain in your life, but it does not make you less in my eyes. It is not by accident, however, that I have allowed you to go through this. It is as, Neal A. Maxwell once said, a 'divine compliment God has given you by placing you here—now' (*Ensign,* Oct. 2004, p. 31) because I knew your pure and precious soul would seek beyond the darkness in your life to find Me. I knew you would not become bitter but purified through this. You had the faith to turn to Me to help you through this refiner's fire. I love you infinitely, beyond anything you could know or experience in this life. You will come to taste of that love more and more. Because you've built your foundation on Me, no matter what happens in this life—no matter the trials, afflictions and adversities that come to you—you can have peace, comfort and wholeness in Me. Your wholeness will bless the others around you as you lead them to Me, as well. Do you know your special strength and intrinsic worth? I love you infinitely and eternally, and I will never forsake you."

"For a Time Such as This" (Esther 4:14)

Truly, many righteous women and men have "come to the kingdom for such a time as this" (Esther 4:14) to help cleanse sin and iniquity from the kingdom of God and prepare the earth for the Lord's second coming. These missions to cleanse are often foreordained special missions the Lord has assigned to chosen sons and daughters whom He knew would be faithful to Him. Carlfred Broderick, in his article entitled "The Uses of Adversity," describes this concept. He sets forth two situations which beautifully illustrate the special calling many righteous souls have been given at this time in the earth's history. He states:

> . . .Two stories were extraordinarily instructive to me. They both came through opportunities I had as a stake president to give blessings. Often the Lord has taught me through blessings; as I've had my hands on someone's head, He's taught me things I did not know and sometimes didn't want to know. The first one was a case of a sister whom I'd known for years and who, in my judgment, had made some very poor life choices. She had married a handsome, charming young man who initially wasn't a member of the Church but joined the Church for her. She waited a year to marry him and then went to the temple. It was the last time he ever went to the temple. I knew he was a flake from the beginning. Out of my wisdom, it didn't surprise me that he soon returned to many of his pre-Church habits—most of the transgressions in the book that you can think of and some that I might not have.
>
> There was great pain for this woman. A good,

good woman, she kept in the Church; she kept in the kingdom; she suffered enormous pain because her husband went back to gambling and drinking and other things that were unhappy and unwholesome. But, the greater pain came when her children, having these two models before them, began to follow him. He would say things like, "Well, you can go to church with your mother and sit through three hours of you know what, or you can come to the racetrack with me, and we'll have good stuff to eat and drink and have a great time." It was a tough choice, and very often the children chose to go with him. They gradually seemed to adopt his lifestyle, values, and attitude toward the Church and toward sacred things. Although she never wavered from her own faith and faithfulness and her commitment to her Heavenly Father, her family was slipping away from her.

As she asked me for a blessing to sustain her in what to do with this awful situation in which she found herself, my thoughts were, "Didn't you ask for this? You married a guy who really didn't have any depth to him and raised your kids too permissively. You should have fought harder to keep them in the church rather than letting them run off to racetracks." I had all those judgments in my head. I laid my hands on her head, and *the Lord told her of His love and His tender concern for her. He acknowledged that He had given her (and that she had volunteered for) a far, far harder task than He would like.* (And, as He put in my mind, a harder task than I had had. I have eight good kids, the last of whom just went to the temple. All would have been good if they had been orphans.) *She, however, had signed up for hard children, for children who had rebellious spirits but who were valuable; for a hard husband who had a rebellious spirit but who was valuable.* The Lord alluded to events in her life that I hadn't known about, but which she confirmed afterwards: twice Heavenly Father had given her the choice between life and death, whether to come home and be relieved of her responsibilities, which weren't going very well, or whether to stay to see if she could work them through. Twice on death's bed she had sent the messenger away and gone back to that hard task. She stayed with it.

I repented. *I realized I was in the presence of one of the Lord's great noble spirits, who had chosen not a safe place behind the lines pushing out the ordinance to the people in the front lines as I was doing, but somebody who chose to live out in the trenches where the Lord's work was being done, where there was risk, where you could be hurt, where you could lose, where you could be destroyed by your love. That's the way she had chosen to labor.* Then I thought; "I am unworthy to lay my hands on her head; if our sexes were reversed, she should have had her hands on mine."

Now she is doing well. . . .I know that she risked her life for service. In a blessing the Lord said to her, "When you're in my employ, the wages are from me, not from those you serve."

In the second case I had a woman who came to me who was an incest victim—the victim of a terrible family. She was abused physically. Her mother was neurotic and stayed in bed all the time to get her daughter to do all the work, including taking care of the husband's needs when he was drunk. The daughter had been abused in about every way there was to be abused—psychologically, physically, sexually. Besides that she had to do all the housework.

She was not a member of the Church at that time, although this happens to members of the Church also. In high school she met a young man who was a Latter-day Saint and who started taking her to church with him. Eventually they married. He was gentle and kind and patient because she didn't come with very many positive attitudes toward men, marital intimacy, or many other things. But he was long-suffering and patient and loved her. They raised some boys.

Despite this, she had recurring bouts of depression and very negative feelings about herself because she had been taught by the people most important in her early life what a rotten person she was. It was hard for her to overcome that self-image. I worked with her to build her self-image. One day she said to me, "You're a stake president." She wasn't in my stake, but she said, "You're a stake president; you explain to me the justice of it." She said, "I go to church and I can hardly stand it. When I see little girls being hugged and kissed and taken to church and appropriately loved by their fathers and mothers, I just want to get up and leave. I say, 'Heavenly Father, what was so terrible about me that, when I was that age, I didn't get any of that? What did that little girl do in the premortal existence that I didn't do so she is loved, so she is safe? Her daddy gives her priesthood blessings when she's sick. Her mother loves her and supports her and teaches her. What did I do? Can you tell me that God is just if He sends that little girl to that family and me to my family?'" She said, "It's a good thing I had boys. I don't think I could have stood to raise girls and have their father love them because I'm so envious."

I would not have known how to answer her in my own capacity because that is manifestly unjust. Where here or in eternity is the justice in an innocent child's suffering in that way? But the Lord inspired me to tell her, and I believe with all my heart that it applies to any in the kingdom, that *she was a valiant Christ-like spirit who volunteered (with, I told her, perhaps too much spiritual pride) to come to earth and suffer innocently to purify a lineage. She volunteered to absorb the poisoning of sin, anger, anguish, and violence, to take it into herself and not to pass it on; to purify a lineage so that downstream from her it ran pure and clean, full of love and the Spirit of the Lord and self-worth. I believed that truly her calling was to be a savior on Mount Zion: That is, to be Savior-like, like the Savior, to suffer innocently that others might not suffer. She voluntarily took such a task with the promise she would not be left alone and abandoned, but He would send one to take her by the hand and be her companion out into the light. I viewed that woman in a different way also, again realizing I was in the presence of one of the great ones and unworthy to have my hands on her head."* (Stovall/Madsen, *As Women of Faith,* 1989, pp. 110-111, italics added)

The Lord allows precious sons and daughters to go through daunting trials—not because He loves them less but because He knows that the spiritual strength and stamina they gain by remaining true and faithful to Him through them is everlasting, "for our light affliction, which is but for a moment, worketh for us a far more exceeding and eternal weight of glory." (2nd Corinthians 4:17) Opposition is truly what causes us to grow in this life. As with weight lifting, the heavier the opposition, the more strength and stamina gained. There is no growth without opposition.

The Savior does not leave those going through opposition alone, however. He promises those who are planted in "a poor spot of ground" that he will "nourish. . .it this long time" (Jacob 5:22)—that is, take extra special care and watch over that spot of ground even more closely—with unvarying attention. He promises to especially watch over those who are planted in a "spot of ground. . .poorer than the first" (Jacob 5:23)—those with even greater difficulties and trials. He will send strength, light and protection to them; He will send insights, comfort, guidance and reassurance. He will never abandon His sons and daughters but promises to "not leave (them) comfortless." (John 14:18)

One woman said, "I would never have chosen to go through what I've had to go through. The pain of it all was horrendous. But I would never trade the growth and strength I have today from what I've experienced. I've learned to base my life on my Savior in a way I never have before. I feel more peace and strength in my life. I've learned to value myself and my efforts instead of feeling so insecure. I had such low self-esteem before and didn't feel that my needs and views were valid—or important. Now that I know of my Savior's pure love for me, it fills me with a completeness that is beyond anything I've ever had. I've tasted His pure patience and tender love in very real ways. I don't think I would have experienced this unless I had to go through the trials I've faced."

Another woman said, "I was told in a priesthood blessing that the Lord allowed me to go through heavy trials in my life because I wouldn't have grown as much as I needed to during my mortal existence if I had not been put through them. He said I had been given burdens and trials so I could stretch instead of skimming through life, as I would have done had these things not happened to me." This is true for many choice souls who are going through tremendous trials and burdens. The Lord is allowing them to grow in Him, letting their souls become purified and refined as they turn to Him for strength and guidance.

9

"The Lord God Will Disperse the Powers of Darkness From Before You" (D&C 21:6): Healing a Wounded Heart

Just as there are certain key elements for transgressors to understand to change and truly repent, so are there principles that will help those they have been hurt heal from their wounds and become whole and strong in the Savior. Those principles are as follows:

"Touch not their unclean things." (Alma 5:57) So often when the adversary presents solutions to problems that have occurred because of sexual sin, he will entice those victimized to engage in sin to find their wholeness, as well. Instead of salving their pain, however, their hurts and wounds only increase. For example, one woman whose husband had an affair on her chose to have an affair, as well, "since I was hurting so much and this was one way I could feel loved." Instead of greater healing, however, she experienced further pain and devastation. Others will choose to engage in damaging practices—like participation in pornography with their husbands, for example, to try and retain their husband's interest. Many engage in demeaning sexual intimacy, as well, as an attempt to arrest deviant behaviors of their partners—hoping their submission will result in their partners not straying. As

mentioned previously, the adversary's solutions will only hurt and harm further. The only true way to healing is based on following the Savior and His ways—turning to Him for wholeness and no one—and nothing—else.

To those victims who have chosen to sin to heal their own wounds, there is hope. The Savior offers the same love, tenderness and mercy as he does to those of His other lost sheep who have transgressed. He wants to heal His wounded sheep so that they may "be gathered unto me a righteous people, without spot and blameless." (D&C 38:31) He has the power and capacity to do this. He doesn't do this angrily, judgmentally or critically. He does it lovingly and tenderly. He knows of the hurts, damages and heartaches that have led to the inward gaping holes transgressors have been trying to fill. He understands their struggles and pains. He knows their heavy trials and afflictions—the darkness, discouragement and oppression they've felt. He understands it fully. He tenderly walks with these souls through their burdens and sorrows, healing them inwardly—and lastingly—through His grace, love and infinite power.

Though those who have transgressed must suffer the buffetings of the adversary as part of the breaking of eternal law— since there is "a law given, and a punishment affixed" (Alma 42:20) for those broken laws, the Savior knows of the trials that have come unfairly to them and will thus reach out and extend "His merciful arm" (Alma 29:10) that much further. He promises, "I will be merciful unto you; he that is weak among you hereafter shall be made strong." (D&C 50:16)

One woman said, "I always felt so awful because of my choice to sin (after her husband's betrayal). I wanted to clean up my life and feel worthy again but always felt so bad about what I'd done. I hated the fact that I had participated in the very things that had hurt me. The Lord helped me and brought me to where I am today. He let me know that through my repentance, I was clean before Him and that I was learning the things He desired me to learn. When I was thinking about Eve one day, the Lord impressed on my mind how it was through her transgression that she came to understand the Savior and the joy of her redemption. It is through my transgressions that I have learned the same things in my life. I know I am a daughter of God and that He loves me. Through His Son I have become whole."

Satan would have God's sons and daughters feel as if they can never become clean and virtuous if they've made mistakes. But the Savior "hath power given unto him from the Father to redeem (his people) from their sins because of repentance; therefore he hath sent his angels to declare the tidings of the conditions of repentance, which bringeth unto the power of the Redeemer, unto the salvation of their souls." (Helaman 5:11)

This experience is a "chapter" in a book; it is not the whole book. One of Satan's greatest tools to afflict and torment innocent souls is to make them think the burdens, pains, heartaches and sorrows they're experiencing from others' terrible choices will never go away—that they will always feel crippling pain, devastation, hurt, darkness and sorrow. Though the pain that comes is deep and as John Taylor described, may "wrench our very heartstrings," (*Journal of Discourses,* 14:360) it will not be lasting. When the Savior becomes part of the equation, there is healing. Little by little and day by day there will be increased light, renewed hope and rebuilt strength—even when there are times that occur that make this seem impossible.

Many injured souls can testify that this kind of healing is possible. One woman said, "After my husband left me (because of his deep sexual addiction and subsequent affair with another woman), I thought I would never be happy again. Today I have relatively nothing and yet I'm happier than I've ever been." Another woman said that in the initial stages of her grief, "I hurt so much I felt I wanted to leave this existence and go home to our Father in Heaven. I couldn't bear the pain I was feeling. Now I marvel at the strength I've gained from my Savior. I feel independent of the hurt that once crushed me. It's a miracle to me that I feel the way I do knowing how I used to feel and how broken I was. I'm so grateful for the spiritual freedom I have now."

Another woman described the time in which she felt the

pain and burdens she kept experiencing would never go away. In a priesthood blessing she sought to deal with her situation, the Lord told her that the adversary had taken a "magnifying glass" and placed it in front of her eyes so that all her burdens, trials and heartaches seemed insurmountable—they appeared to be mountains instead of "boulders." He promised her that through Him the magnifying glass would be taken away and that she would see her problems for what they were. He promised those rocks would be chipped away and taken care of—piece by piece—until they no longer thwarted her path.

Through the Savior those wounded can gain independence from everything and everyone in this world—except the Savior Himself. This applies to everyone, even if broken relationships are not healed and spouses are left alone.

Those closest can inflict the most pain and hurt. One of the most sobering realities of facing betrayal because of sexual sin is that the deeper someone has loved, the more pain that person will feel from a betrayal. There will be countless tears, anguish, turmoil, misery, sorrow, suffering and torment that occur. As one woman described an impression from the Lord during the devastation of a heavy trial, "The pain goes as deep and as far as the love." (Duncan, *Ensign,* April 1996, p. 24)

As hurtful as it is, facing and experiencing the pain is part of the healing process. Keeping that pain inside will only hurt, canker and damage souls even further. Part of effectively dealing with pain is being able to share that pain in a safe environment. It must be shared and expressed fully to be overcome—often over and over again through the entire process of healing.

Though pain must be worked through whether or not a relationship heals, the eventual healing of a relationship requires being able to completely share painful emotions with the person who caused them. It must be remembered that such a circumstance will *never* happen initially but will only come about through time and through the true repentance of a transgressor. The key to reaching that point is finding the correct environment in which to share pain initially—so one can survive the turmoil and anguish sexual sin has brought about in their lives.

Safe environments to share pain may include ecclesiastical leaders, support groups, counselors, special friends, close family members or others the Lord plants in lives to assist in the healing process. Keeping a journal often helps, as well. One woman described how a support group became her place to share her trials because "no one knew my last name or who my husband was. I could share the hard realities of what my husband had participated in without it hurting either of us. I don't know what I would have done if I didn't have this place to unload. I needed to talk it all out. It was my lifeline." Another woman said, "I never realized that when I moved into my new ward that Heavenly Father had women there who would help me through my husband's leaving me (because of infidelity). They had gone through similar trials and understood my experiences. I don't know what I would have done without them."

People going through intense trials could be compared to water pots. The events of their lives are like drops of water that fill them—sometimes quickly, when there are great torrents of burdens or pains, and sometimes slowly, like the slow drops of normal activities in life. If there is a safe "garden" to pour out these emotions and experiences, everything will run better and the pot will be more able to handle life's flow. However, if emotions and experiences are bottled up, soon they can overflow in unrestrained emotion and cause damage. There must be safe places to pour out the events of life in order to move forward effectively.

It should be remembered that in seeking safe environments in which to express feelings and emotions, those who do so need to seek for persons who worthily represent the Lord and His righteousness. People who do not follow the Lord's Spirit can often be tools of the adversary to afflict and harm souls further with false ideas and teachings. For example, one woman who had an affair counseled with a close family member regarding her choice to participate in adultery. That family member told her that she had been justified in her behaviors because her husband had never known how to treat her correctly and fulfill her needs. He said that because of his lacks he never would—and she had thus been justified in not wanting her relationship and looking outside it for fulfillment. These words and ideas did not move the woman toward healing but trapped her further in her misery and self-justification, making it even harder to heal herself and her marriage.

As a further caution, even those who worthily represent the Lord can be misled in their thinking occasionally. That is why it is so essential to never put trust "in the arm of flesh" (2nd Nephi 4:24) but the Lord only. For example, one woman and her husband went in to receive counseling from a Stake President for serious marital problems. Unbeknownst to anyone at that time, the husband was participating in deep sexual sin that included topless bars and prostitution. During that appointment, the husband proceeded to tear his wife apart—criticizing her for her lack of love toward him physically, emotionally and mentally.

After hearing the husband's complaints, the Stake President lovingly chastised the wife, telling her that she needed to get on her knees and pray to "cherish" her husband as a wife should. The majority of the blame for the problems was placed on her. She went home broken, defeated and heartbroken—and felt completely overcome by the loneliness she felt. When the sins of her husband later came to light, she could see how her husband's warped and twisted thinking had influenced a righteous man to think in similar ways. Though she trusted that leader's efforts and intents to follow the Savior, in that instance she felt he had been misled by the lies told to him by her husband. This can happen to anyone. It is therefore the Savior's approval—and His only—that one should seek to obtain, no one else's.

Learning to Discern Truth in a Network of Lies. One of the hardest trials that exists when dealing with those who have been involved in sexual transgression is learning to discern undiluted truth in a network of lies. Transgressors who have participated in sexual sin have inevitably adopted lies—and told lies—to justify their behaviors, actions and attitudes. Transgressors' lies often form a complex, confusing web that is extremely difficult—and sometimes impossible—to unravel.

Part of what makes discerning truth so difficult when sexual sin has occurred is that transgressors often believe their lies and deceptions are "truths." They have literally become blind to "things as they are, and as they were, and as they are to come" (D&C 93:24). Korihor, in the *Book of Mormon*, is a perfect example of this. He taught Satan's lies because "they were pleasing to the carnal mind," (Alma 30:53) insomuch that he caused many to "lift up their heads in their wickedness" and "commit whoredoms." (Alma 30:18) Korihor taught these lies, again and again, until he "verily believed that they were true." (Alma 30:53) His lies became "truths" to him, although his "truths" were false, skewed and distorted perceptions of reality.

This is where problems exist for those working with transgressors. Often someone can discern another's telling of falsehood when falsehood is spoken as falsehood. But when someone actually speaks falsehood as "truth," it is far harder to discern and disbelieve. Only seeing and understanding clearly the truth will free outside parties from being subjected to transgressors' lies and deceptions.

For example, one woman said that whenever she talked to her ex-husband, who had filed for divorce from her because of his adulterous relationship with another woman, she would have to "step back and try to clear my head. I would get caught up in what he said and his string of lies—especially his accusations about me. He would tell me how messed up I was and how I was the one who created all the problems in our marriage. I could feel myself buying into his thinking and I would have to stop myself. It was so hard to not accept his rationale as truth."

One woman spoke of the time when, after severe marital strains in her marriage, she confronted her husband about whether or not he had an addiction to pornography. He resentfully told her "no" without any hesitation, openly scoffing at the idea. Because of his reactions, she decided to take his word for it. Several years later, however, she discovered that her husband's sexual problems had led him to an ongoing two-year affair with another woman, an affair which only stopped because of her discovery of it.

As another example, one man came in alone to counsel with his bishop regarding marital problems he and his wife were experiencing. During the course of the conversation, the bishop asked him directly if he had any problem with pornography or other sexual sins. He responded with a firm, "No." Upon further questioning, however, the bishop discovered this man had viewed pornography scarcely the night before. This man's constant viewing of pornography—since a teen—soon after came out, yet he still did not believe himself addicted or as having a problem with pornography. This man's "confession," then, of not having any sexual problems was—in his mind—truthful and honest. It took him a long time after this encounter to begin see that he had an addiction and then to seek help in overcoming it.

Philip A. Harrison in his book, *Clean Hands, Pure Heart,* said this regarding the deception that accompanies sexual transgression: "Lies are the basis of all the evil in the world. Every person who indulges in sin has accepted the lie that happiness can be found in sin. In the midst of addiction, I wandered in a fog of lies—lies I believed, as well as lies I told. Before I could get free from addiction, I needed to become free from these damaging falsehoods that I both believed and acted upon." (p. 37)

For those working with transgressors, they, too, need to become free from the "damaging falsehoods" of the past and learn to discern truth accurately. Part of this means coming to clearly see where lies were told and to what degree—and then refusing to put up with continuing lies, skewed reasoning behind those lies and further justification for those lies. This takes courage, strength, commitment and determination, especially since transgressors often attack those who try to uncover lies as contentious, vengeful, critical, deceptive or hypocritical.

One woman said, "When I learned of my husband's (deep sexual addiction), it took me a long time to separate what I had believed about our past to what had truly happened in our marriage. I had to face some bitter truths. I had felt we had a foundation of fidelity and trust; we did not. I had believed he was committed and faithful to me; he was not. Part of what became so hard working through this is that he did not see what he'd done as seriously as I did—or that it destroyed the foundation of our relationship. When he first confessed to (a sexual problem), he told me he hadn't crossed the line in being unfaithful to me. I had believed him. As more time went on and the full truth finally came out as to what my husband had participated in, I became astounded at the depth he'd reached. He had been unfaithful—many, many times. I couldn't believe he had claimed he 'hadn't crossed the line' because he had. I couldn't believe he felt faithful and committed to me because he had not been—for years."

She continued, "I had to learn to trust my perceptions of the past and what I felt—never his perceptions or how he viewed it. His perceptions were tainted and he did not take his mistakes as seriously as I did. I had to hold firmly to my convictions regarding what had happened because he rationalized and always made things appear less than what they were. Because I'd believed him in the past—and had believed his lies, I had been deceived for a long time. It took me a long time to learn to sift through what he said."

Transgressors truly have based their realities on false ideas, deceptions and untruths. As Laurie Hall stated in her book, *An Affair of the Mind*, "Most sex addicts are pathological liars. They lie about everything, not just their sexual behavior, and they do so with straight faces. They lie when telling the truth would save them time and money. They lie to themselves about what they're doing. They lie to their wives and families about where they're going and what they're going to do when they get there, even if there's no sexually inappropriate behavior going on."

She then concludes, "When we lie, . . .we deliberately take ourselves out of the light and plunge ourselves into the darkness. When we walk in darkness, we are walking in Satan's jurisdiction." (pp. 117-118)

Until transgressors learn to speak and live based on everlasting truth, they will not heal—nor will the relationships surrounding them heal. All relationships based on any form of deception cannot last; they will be like the great and spacious building seen by Nephi and Lehi—without foundation, thus causing "the fall thereof" to be "exceedingly great." (1 Nephi 11:36)

The Willingness to Not Tell Truth is a Lie. So often transgressors have justified living lives of deception by simply not telling the truth—or telling a "truth" based on their false realities. Withholding truth is another form of lying. This can be illustrated in the following true example. A police officer who had worked for years with domestic abuse cases would often be called upon the scene after domestic violence had taken place. Sometimes, even when a woman would appear with cuts or bruises after an altercation, he would ask the perpetrator of the crime, "Did you hit your wife?" Most often he would get the answer, "No." This officer learned to question a perpetrator in different ways. He would continue, "Did you slap your wife? Did you push her? Did you shove her? Did you touch her in any way?" Only by doing this could he uncover the truth of what had happened. In perpetrators' minds, then, the question, "Did you hit your wife?" could be answered truthfully by them as "no" if they'd "slapped" or "shoved" or "pushed."

So often this kind of withholding of truth happens with transgressors. For example, one transgressor had been asked if he had been unfaithful to his wife. He said, "No." Upon further questioning, it was discovered that he'd had repeated encounters with prostitutes over many years. He had justified himself as being faithful because he had never committed the final act of adultery. He did not see everything leading up to that act as being "unfaithful" and had drawn a distorted, skewed perception of truth. Yet in his mind, he had been telling the truth.

As another example, when it came to issues of moral cleanliness, one ecclesiastical leader learned to question those who came into his office in greater depth. Instead of asking, "Are you morally pure?" or "Do you have any problems with immorality?" he would ask more direct questions. He would ask, for example, "When was the last time you viewed pornography?" If he received an affirmative answer, he would question someone additionally.

"Did that pornographic site come to you or did you purposefully seek it?" This leader uncovered countless problems with moral cleanliness because of the way he had learned to question those that came to him—those who believed they were telling the truth but were glossing, telling half-truths or purposefully hiding.

"We Should Bring. . .to Light all the Hidden Things of Darkness." (D&C 123:13) More often than not, transgressors choose to keep hidden the darkness in their lives because of sexual sin and it is others that have to bring truth out. Satan is cunning in his attempts to justify transgressors keeping their sins hidden. He whispers such things as, "You really didn't fall. What you did is a normal part of being human—a normal part of life. Keep it to yourself. You needn't tell anyone." Or, "Telling your wife would only hurt her, and you love her and are committed to her. You wouldn't want her to bear the burden of this. Keep it to yourself; keep it secret. You love her too much to hurt her in this way. Besides, you won't do it again, anyway. You've repented because you're committed to not doing it again." Or, "You really didn't cross the line. You pulled away just in time. Look how good you did in pulling away before anything truly serious happened. You're completely okay; you're completely justified. Don't feel bad; you're fine."

Darkness, lies, secrecy and deception are the result of sexual sin. Often those on the outside are the ones who have to determine whether or not there are these kinds of problems occurring in relationships and then bring those problems to light. Most often the greatest determining factor of knowing when one needs to uncover darkness is the still, small voice inside that whispers, "Something is just not right here. I don't know what it is, but what is happening just doesn't settle well with me. This behavior is confusing and puzzling to me."

The most common issue that contributes to this inward, unsettled feeling is ongoing contention and anger in relationships—anger that isn't easily eradicated, overcome or worked through. Transgressors become angry, moody, and contentious and are easily offended at little things others do or say. Others working with them are often confused at how upset and frustrated they get over seemingly inconsequential things. Manipulation, control, put-downs and fault-finding are other fruits that cause this feeling, as well. Secretiveness; increased time away from home; changes in intimacy; and changes in spirituality are other signs.

There are other signs that are common threads that may be indicative of sexual sin. One private investigator told a woman that he could often tell when infidelity had occurred in a relationship by certain outside indicators. These included: 1) A change of lifestyle. There often was a sudden care about appearance that included behaviors such as tanning, weight loss, joining a gym, preoccupation with dressing and clothes, and so forth. 2) Purchases. Usually there are large, extravagant purchases by transgressors for only them—purchases designed for self-gratification or pleasure. These purchases include such items as a large-screen TVs, automobiles, bikes, boats and so on. 3) Money. There exists a change in the handling of money, particularly where money is hidden somewhere. This would include such things as new accounts or increased, unexplained withdrawals. 4) Secrecy. They become secretive about their whereabouts and are usually gone a lot, including late at night. And finally, 5) Changes with intimacy. With infidelity comes a change in sexual habits with a partner. This may include things such as experimentation or other actions. Sometimes intimacy decreases or becomes non-existent. These were all outside "signs" that the private investigator had learned to recognize to indicate that sexual problems were occurring.

Our Savior has told us that he "worketh not in darkness." (2 Nephi 26:23) In His own way and in His own timing, He will bring "hidden things. . .to light" (Mosiah 8:17) when His faithful sons and daughters turn to Him in pleading prayer to bring this about in their lives. It is only when sin and darkness are brought out and exposed to His light that they can even begin to be overcome.

Dealing with the Pain of Deception. Many people have spoken of the deep pain that comes from having been deceived—deep pain that is independent of the betrayal committed in a relationship. One woman said, "When I discovered my husband's deception and lies to me throughout our marriage, it felt as devastating to me as his infidelity. I suddenly felt invalidated as a person in his eyes. To him, I was not worthy of respect or someone he needed to remain truthful to. The fact that he lied to me repeatedly felt as hurtful and devastating to me as knowing he had betrayed me physically. My heart ached and I felt essentially worthless to him—since he was willing to do that to me and treat me in that way. I felt devastated that my trust in him had been treated so lightly. I had come into my marriage wanting to be loved and cherished—and have the full commitment of my partner. I was not given those things. The hurt from that kind of deception is agonizing."

Many have spoken about the pain that comes from the lies and deception of transgressors. Turning to the Savior, once again, for security and strength is the only way someone can survive not feeling validated and valued—especially when lies and deception have occurred over many, many years. New realities have to be created for victims, too, as they sift through the past to discern the truth as to what happened—and thus build a new foundation based on truth, not what they believed was truth.

"No matter what spiritual things I do, I feel heavy darkness and oppression. Nothing seems to help rid the darkness from my life." The darkness that is a result of sexual sin is heavy and oppressive. Learning to discern it and overcome it is an essential part of moving toward healing—but it occurs over a lengthy process of time, not quickly or immediately. The daily spiritual feeding of souls—sincere prayer, scripture study, consistent temple attendance, attending church meetings and so forth—is a fundamental element of overcoming darkness. Stopping these because of not feeling immediate fruits is like not watering seeds because no green foliage has risen above the earth; to stop means the seeds would wither and die. Such it would be with stopping spiritual efforts. Souls would wither and die from lack of proper nutrients.

The Lord has made promises to each of us that He will not

leave us "comfortless" but will "come" to us. (John 14:18) That means He will pierce the heavy clouds of darkness surrounding struggling souls to send rays of comfort and hope—in different ways for each person. One of the most powerful tools of hearing His voice through heavy burdens is receiving blessings through His Holy Priesthood. The Lord can then speak directly to an anguished soul in need of comfort, assurance, strength and direction.

Many, many people going through the intense trials pertaining to sexual sin have needed consistent and ongoing priesthood blessings to stay afloat. One woman said, "The only way I survived (my trials) was by turning to the priesthood for blessings and strength. I was in so much turmoil that sometimes this was the only way I could hear the Lord's voice. I never stopped my prayers or scripture reading, but sometimes my mind felt so confused and burdened that I didn't always get out of those what I had previously. When the Lord would speak to me through priesthood blessings, I had enough faith to recognize His voice and continue forward, even though I struggled hearing His voice through my own efforts. I thank Him that He gave me this comfort. I don't think I would have made it through my trials otherwise."

The Lord desires all of His children to have access to the blessings of His restored church. To those struggling through burdens and heartaches who don't have the blessings of the priesthood nearby, through prayers of faith they can often be given to them—through ecclesiastical leaders, friends, extended family, home teachers or so forth. If not, the Lord will assuredly prepare other ways to receive comfort and strength. One woman said she "often felt the ministering of angels" when she needed comfort and could not gain it through priesthood blessings. Others have moments of peace and light accompanied by clarity of mind they haven't felt for a long time. Others have friends or counselors who speak words of wisdom and truth to them that bring comfort and peace. The Lord will never abandon His children when they turn to Him, even if in the dark mists they don't feel Him as readily.

"I feel so needy and insecure because of what has happened to me. I'm not sure I'll ever stop feeling this way."

Many times after betrayals, there are continued insecurities that resurface in relationships that stymie confidence and trust in rebuilding and healing—whether or not transgressors are sincerely trying to repent. For example, one woman said that during the process of trying to rebuild her marriage, "whenever my husband and I got along for a few days, I always felt so insecure that it would not last. I would quickly withdraw emotionally from him if I felt the slightest hint of distance on his part. Sometimes I felt like I wanted and needed constant verbal reassurance—'I love you' or 'I'm sorry for what I did.' Sometimes I wanted continual physical shows of love from him. I never dared ask, though. I could not bear the thought of being turned down. I couldn't stand further betrayal, even on a tiny level, again. I just felt so insecure and vulnerable in all aspects of our relationship. Whenever I felt like this, I had to pray to my Savior once again for the reassurance I was looking for instead of turning to my husband—who may or may not give it to me. Despite where my husband was at in our relationship, I knew I could feel safe and reassured with my Savior no matter what. So, if I ever felt shaky and insecure, I would quickly turn to Him to feel safe and whole again."

All thus struggling need to find their wholeness and security from their relationship with the Savior to give them the sustenance and confidence they need—instead of looking for it in others, even repentant partners in marriages or others outside marriages. It is when this happens that the smaller insecurities and vulnerabilities will melt away because "then shall (their) confidence wax strong in the presence of God" (D&C 121:45) and become unshakable.

This concept is true for those who end up alone after betrayals, as well. Security and strength must be gained from the Savior. One woman said pertaining to this, "I was so afraid to date because I felt so insecure. I felt like I would have taken anyone that came along who showed me love. As I gained more faith in my Savior, it was amazing to see how much stronger I got in my interactions with others. I didn't feel like I needed to get approval or attention. It brought greater depth into the relationships I did have and actually weeded out a few that would have probably not have been good for me."

Truly, the Savior can become the "rock" of a strong and steady "foundation" (Helaman 5:12) for anyone trying to heal from the damage of sexual sin. It is through His strength—and His alone—that hearts are mended, confidence is regained and trust is renewed in relationships. He needs to become the foundation and keystone of relationships in order for them to become lasting and eternal.

Righteously sticking up for oneself—or one's ideas— firmly and defensively during discussions or confrontations is not contentious or angry; it is essential to wholeness. Another way Satan afflicts and torments victims of betrayals is by convincing them that they are not following the Savior—that they are not forgiving, loving and Christ-like—if they boldly or firmly defend or express themselves during verbal confrontations, arguments or discussions. It is essential to emotional wholeness and wellbeing to set forth and defend what one believes is righteous and true—even if a person is attacked as being contentious, blind, hypocritical or mean-spirited by doing so. Allowing someone to verbally demean, afflict or manipulate—without defending oneself or removing oneself from that situation—is not what the Lord intends for His sons and daughters. This is not to say the Lord condones vengeful, angry or abusive attacks in return, but He never expects someone to subject themselves to emotional pain or abuse in their "forgiveness" or attempts to meekly follow the Savior.

Kendal Hunter in his book, *Consider My Servant Job,* talks about Job's experience that helps give insight in this regard. He asked the question, "Wasn't Job being arrogant and contentious in defending himself [to his friends]? Aren't we supposed to be meek and longsuffering in our trials?"

He answered in this way:

> As to being arrogant, we have a right to defend our good name (TPJS 341). In fact, if Job did not defend himself, we would assume that he was guilty. The rule is, "Silence gives consent." If he remained silent, he

would have consented to their slanders.

. . .As to being contentious, when Christ spoke about contention, he was referring to contentions about doctrine (3 Nephi 11:29). Job, on the other hand, was defending his good name, which is a different matter.

As to being humble in his trials, Job was very humble before his trials, he was humble during his trials, and remained humble to the end of his trials. Humility is not being a pushover, but submitting to God. Christ was meek and lowly (Matthew 11:29), but he was not so tender that he could not deliver a sharp rebuke when needed. (See Matthew 23). He even once referred to Peter as Satan (Mosiah 8:33).

Joseph Smith explained the meaning of "meek and lowly":

Some of the company thought I was not a very meek Prophet, so I told them: "I am meek and lowly in heart," and will personify Jesus for a moment, to illustrate the principle, and cried out with a loud voice, "Woe unto you, ye doctors; woe unto you, ye lawyers; woe unto you, ye scribes, Pharisees, and hypocrites!" But you cannot find the place where I ever went that I found fault with their food, their drink, their house, their lodgings; no, never; and this is what is meant by the meekness and lowliness of Jesus (TPJS, 270)."

Kendall Hunter then concludes, "We have an obligation to defend our good name, since it reflects upon ourselves, our family and the church. . . .This is not contending about doctrine, but the boldest speaking of truth." (pp. 45-46) Thus it is with defending one's self during arguments or confrontations. Firmly holding on to or defending ideas and opinions—and not putting up with abuse or attacks—is a righteous and meek way of following the Savior; it is not vicious and contentious—even if one is blamed for being so by doing it.

Healing Intimacy. A heart-wrenching challenge to healing relationships scarred by sexual sin is finding safety, security and fulfillment in intimacy. Just as healing anything after deep devastation takes a great deal of time, healing intimacy also takes time and comes "line upon line, precept upon precept: here a little, and there a little." (D&C 128:21) Many people who have been betrayed, however, can speak of the healing that comes to them when they turn to the Savior in these delicate matters.

One woman spoke of her experience as follows: "I felt so shaken about intimacy after I found out about my husband (and his infidelity). I didn't know what to do. Everything in our relationship was crushed and destroyed, including that. I felt so confused. I didn't know what to do to move forward or if I could ever love (my husband) freely again, without feeling the act was desecrated. I know Heavenly Father sustained me. I would plead to Him to help me not feel vulnerable. Sometimes He would give me increased desire, or other times He helped me verbally express my hurt to my husband about opening up myself to him in that way. I was not left alone through any of it. With something so sensitive and close to the heart, Heavenly Father will not abandon us—ever."

Each person needs to approach the tender feelings surrounding the healing of intimacy differently. One woman spoke of the time she had to have a period of abstinence to regain the personal ground she needed to feel safe in participating in intimacy once again, not giving in to her husband and his "insistent demands." Another had to leave the home for awhile "so I didn't feel pressure to stay and participate in something I feel I could not do at the time. I felt too hurt. I needed to get away so I could make decisions about our relationship without that kind of pressure hanging over my head." Another woman spoke of how intimacy helped her feel more secure in her relationship instead of making her feel vulnerable—bringing her strength and comfort, not adding to her wounds.

Each person is different, but each can respectively receive the assurances of the Savior when He tells us, "Let them ask and they shall receive, knock and it shall be opened unto them, and be made known from on high, even by the Comforter, whither they shall go." (D&C 75:27)

***Becoming Aware of the Adversary's Attacks on Women,
Particularly Mothers.*** President Hinckley, in the November 2004
Ensign, stated:

> We see the bitter fruit of th(e) degradation [of
> women] all about us. Divorce is one of the results. This
> evil runs rampant through our society. It is the outcome
> of disrespect for one's marriage partner. It manifests
> itself in neglect, in criticism, in abuse, in abandonment.
> We in the Church are not immune from it.
>
> Jesus declared, "What therefore God hath
> joined together, let not man put asunder" (Matthew
> 19:6).
>
> The word *man* is used in the generic sense, but
> the fact is that *it is predominantly men who bring about
> the conditions that lead to divorce.* (p. 84, italics added)

Truly it is predominantly men that bring about divorce
in their families. So often these divorces are tied to sexual sin
and its devastating consequences. As President Hinckley stated,
women are predominantly the victims, suffering greatly "because
of the wickedness and abominations of their husbands." (Jacob
2:31) Satan attacks these chaste and sensitive souls in countless
ways, but these attacks could be summarized as attacks on 1) what
defines them as a person physically, emotionally, spiritually and
mentally, and 2) their offerings as a person in all aspects of their
lives—as a mother, a sister, a wife, a member of the Church, etc.
As stated previously, these attacks not only come through thoughts
Satan gives but also are often spoken attacks through transgressors'
mouths when transgressors have become instruments and are the
"servants of Satan that do uphold his work." (D&C 10:5)

Mothers and motherhood are particularly attacked, since
righteous mothers are one of the most powerful forces for good
on this earth. Again and again victimized women are heard to say
such things as, "I'm such a bad mother. I feel awful about myself.
I don't do enough for my children. I'm too impatient or angry
with them. I don't help them feel secure. I don't offer enough to

them to help them grow—sports, music lessons, or other activities. I'm too tired and worn out to give them what they need. Because I'm so discouraged and down about my life, I'm so self-absorbed and selfish. I've hurt them because of who I am. I'm such a bad person because of all my struggles and inadequacies. I don't give enough." Intense guilt, lack of self-worth, heavy discouragement and depression are some of the fruits of these thoughts.

The Lord sorrows for His daughters that carry these heavy burdens amongst the other burdens they must carry. He tenderly yearns for them to feel His wholeness and unwavering love—love that will help them redefine who and what they are. They will come to see themselves—through Him—as choice, valiant spirits He has assigned to difficult and arduous missions in this life. The Lord let them face these challenges because He knew their spirits could overcome them with His help and sustaining strength, but He also knew these challenges would take everything they had to give, making it difficult—if not impossible—to give more in other areas of their lives. This does not make them less or substandard to others; they're often carrying burdens that would literally crush others if they had to shoulder the same weight. They truly are valiant, precious gems the Lord guards carefully in His hands and will protect with His might.

Heavenly Father and the Savior will work unceasingly to combat the lies Satan and his servants have told these precious daughters. They will stick up for them firmly, boldly and defensively, for no one "shall lead away captive the daughters of my people because of their tenderness, save I shall visit them with a sore curse, even unto destruction." (Jacob 2:33) Their love and comfort will become a safe haven and be a "refuge from the storm." (D&C 115:6) They will not suffer any attacks on their precious daughters to go unnoticed, but will "be with them even unto the end" (D&C 75:11) and will one day "mete out a just recompense on the heads of all their oppressors." (D&C 127:3)

Children have often come to their homes on earth, too, as valiant, strong soldiers to help their mothers, knowing full well the burdens they would carry because of the unrighteous choices of others. Many children committed before this life to become stripling warriors, helping to defend their families from the enemy. Though in these great battles there will not be "one soul among them who ha(s) not received many wounds," (Alma 57:25) their valiance often shines through the darkness to show their resilience, strength and faith.

The Lord vows to reach out in mercy to His struggling daughters and their children, filling in the gaps for them whenever possible. After all they can do, He asks them to "leave the residue in my hands," (D&C 103:40) promising to sustain them in the areas of their lives where they cannot give more.

This idea can be illustrated by a beautiful story a woman told about the time she attended an event performed by a family in which "all ten children were accomplished, amazing musicians." She said of this experience, "I sat there in awe at what the mother had done in getting them to be where they were at. As the concert went on, I felt worse and worse about myself as a mother and discouraged about what I had not given my own children. I felt tremendous guilt and heartache. As I struggled with these feelings, I prayed to Heavenly Father and asked Him, 'Have I not given my children enough? Have I failed them? Have I made them miss out on life because of who I've been as a mother?'"

The Lord tenderly answered her at this time with a very specific impression. He said to her, "(My daughter), your children came to you because you are the only one on earth who could teach them the things they needed to know. If I need them to learn these other things, I will raise up people to help them."

Each struggling through the ramifications of sexual sin can adopt these promises for themselves, knowing the Lord sent their children to them to learn the things they could learn at no other place or time. He also promises to fill in the gaps in their lives, raising up the people He intends to have help. He is a tender, perfect parent who will uplift, sustain, carry and assist those struggling who turn to Him for help in their trials and burdens

"And Thy Desire Shall be to Thy Husband, and He Shall Rule Over Thee." (Moses 4:22) Our Father in Heaven has planted

in women's hearts special desires toward their husbands. These gifts include things such as wanting to love, support and sustain them, being a "comfort" unto them in their "afflictions, with consoling words, in the spirit of meekness." (D&C 25:5) Women have great capacity to give love, caring and support in this way. These emotions are strong and binding, especially when intimate physical relationships become part of the equation. A woman truly gives her heart and soul—everything intimate and personal—to her husband. She desires to be loved and cherished in return.

Satan takes these divine desires and cruelly twists them when partners in covenant relationships engage in sinful practices. Satan purposefully and cunningly uses transgressors to manipulate the trust, loyalty or commitment their spouses have offered. Often women are made to feel as if they need to take manipulative or abusive behaviors from their husbands in order to maintain peace in their homes. They feel they must support the "patriarchs" and "priesthood leaders"—irrespective of how they are treated in return. They are often hounded with guilt when there is contention and they often take the blame for behaviors that are not theirs but are blamed on them. Other times they will give in to their husbands' demands physically, as if they need to try to meet their desires because "that is what a good wife would do."

For example, one woman spoke of the feeling that she needed to stay with her husband, despite his deep sexual perversions, "because I had married him in the temple. I believed that our relationship was eternal." She says of her experience, "When he started to do perverse things in our marital relationship and expected me to do them with him, I at first went along with it. I felt awful and demeaned. As things progressed, depression set in deeper and deeper. I even contemplated suicide as a means of getting out of my situation. I didn't know what else to do. Then (a family member) felt inspired to rescue me after having the impression that I was being 'destroyed.' (That person) literally came to my rescue, packing me up so I could leave my husband and his abusive behaviors." She attributes this to literally saving her life—and her sanity.

President Gordon B. Hinckley, in the October 2004 General Conference, told the story of a woman whose husband passed away shortly after a deathbed confession to pornography addiction. In her intense emotion, she wrote, "I had brought a pure heart into our marriage, kept it pure during that marriage, and intended to keep it pure ever after. Why could he not do the same for me? All I ever wanted was to feel cherished and treated with the smallest of pleasantries." She concludes, "Pornography. . .has the effect of damaging hearts and souls to their very depths, strangling the life out of relationships that should be sacred, hurting to the very core those you should love the most." (*Ensign,* Nov. 2004, p. 60)

All sexual sin truly has the effect of "damaging hearts and souls to their very depths, strangling the life out of relationships that should be sacred" and "hurting to the core those you should love the most." (Ibid.) Laurie Hall, in her book *An Affair of the Mind,* further illustrates this concept when she spoke about the devastation of pornography. She said:

> Make no mistake—porn kills love. It poisons the heart. It destroys the mind. It deadens the conscience. It literally changes the neural pathways in the brain. It conditions the body to equate sexual arousal with anxiety. It destroys value systems. It destroys respect. It makes you a lousy lover. It is more addictive than cocaine, and it's harder to break than any other addiction. There is no known detox for porn. Unlike alcohol or drugs which will eventually be processed out of the body, once the images of porn are burned into the brain through the potent chemicals that are released when you look at it (especially when masturbation accompanies looking at it), there is no known way to get rid of the images. They keep coming back over and over.
>
> . . .Porn does damage character. It changes the way you think. It makes you slippery and manipulative and irresponsible. It makes you totally self-absorbed and self-centered. It makes you a user of others. Porn destroys the foundations of your life. (pp. 248-249)

When sexual sin occurs in any form whatsoever, this kind of devastation occurs. Women will inevitably be mistreated and devalued in those relationships when they are the victims. Their commitment and loyalties have been betrayed and Satan will do all in his power to use those very traits to damage them further.

Because of this, all women must learn that they have the responsibility to stand up firmly for themselves in their demands for respect. They do not have to put up with belittling behaviors, neglect, criticism, ridicule, abuse or any other types of mistreatment. They have rights to be handled "by persuasion, by long-suffering, by gentleness and meekness, and by love unfeigned; by kindness." (D&C 121:41-42) Only by sticking up for these rights as daughters of God will women begin to heal—whether they stay in marital relationships or not.

This healing process also includes letting the Lord become the one upon which hearts, commitments and loyalties are based. When the Lord spoke to Israel, comparing it to a wife who had been "refused," He said,

> Fear not, for thou shalt not be ashamed; neither be thou confounded, for thou shalt not be put to shame; for thou shalt forget the shame of thy youth, and shalt not remember the reproach of thy widowhood any more.
>
> For thy maker, thy husband, the Lord of Hosts is his name;
>
> . . .For the Lord hath called thee as woman forsaken and a wife of youth, when thou was refused, saith thy God.
>
> For a small moment have I forsaken thee, but with great mercies will I gather thee. (3rd Nephi 22:4-7)

Truly the Lord will gather the brokenhearted with "great mercies" (Ibid.) and heal their deep wounds. Many truly testify of the healing that comes when hearts become centered on the Savior like this, not on husbands who may or may not be faithful. Those who do turn to Him truly come to "receive. . .strength and nourishment form the true vine" (1ˢᵗ Nephi 15:15) and can become whole and strong in His unfailing love.

When Men are Victims of Infidelity. Because the majority of victims of divorce and betrayal are women, those men who have been victimized often do not have the same access to understanding and support as women do. Many feel isolated and alone in their sufferings. Men who have been victims need access to the same kind of sustaining strength and support that women need. They need safe places to share burdens and be sustained in their trials and anguish. Great relief and comfort can be found when burdens are shared instead of being held inside. As one man said after sharing the burdens of his wife's infidelity, "It feels like such a relief to have someone understand what I'm going through—to realize I'm not crazy." This man had to learn that despite his wife's insistence that he not share their marriage problems with others, he needed outside sustenance and support to get through the trials that her infidelity had created between the two of them.

All the Faithful Will Have the Promises of the Faithful. One woman who had gone through difficult trials because of her husband's deep sexual sins said, "As I carried the burdens of my husband's sins, for a great deal of time I felt cheated because I had to go through immense pain and heartache. Some women had been given faithful and loyal partners, but I had not been given this. Some women were happy in their marriages, but I was not. Why? It seemed so unfair. I had tried to remain true and faithful to my covenants, but it hadn't made a difference. My husband was still unfaithful to me."

She continued, "The Lord helped me learn that if I remained faithful to Him—no matter what happened to me in my life, that everything—'all that my Father hath' (D&C 84:38)—would be given to me, too. He promised me in a priesthood blessing that I would not skip out on any blessing that came to the righteous. That meant that one day I, too, would have a loyal and faithful husband— whether it meant my current husband or not, if I remained faithful.

I, too, would be loved and cherished by an eternal companion. I've learned that nothing will be withheld from me if I keep the Savior at the center of my life. This belief has sustained me through my trials. I know that the Lord gives this promise to all of His children going through what I have."

The Lord has stated,

> For what man among you having twelve sons, and is no respecter of them, and they serve him obediently, and he saith unto the one: Be thou clothed in robes and sit thou here; and to the other: Be thou clothed in rags and sit thou there — and looketh upon his sons and saith I am just?
>
> Behold, this I have given unto you as a parable, and it is even as I am. (D&C 38:26)

The Lord is just and perfect and will not withhold any blessing from those who serve Him in righteousness. James E. Faust said pertaining to this, "Some faithful women have been denied that which is at the very center of their souls. In the eternal plan, *no blessing will be kept from the faithful*." (*Ensign,* Nov. 1996, p. 52, italics added) Though women specifically are mentioned in this instance, these blessings also apply to faithful men. No eternal blessing will be held from those who serve the Lord in righteousness and truth.

These faithful souls who have had to go through lives of adversity and challenge because of the choices of others could truly be considered "spiritual pioneers." They have given up lives of comfort and ease on this earth to do a great work of cleansing sin in preparation for the Lord's second coming. Sometimes sexual sin has been passed down from generation to generation but will be stopped because of the righteous and valiant choices of those who remain true to our Savior.

Those who do this kind of cleansing have often been foreordained by our Father and Savior to do this work and help others become whole again. Those left alone after sexual sin who raise children in righteousness or continue in personal lives of righteousness are spiritual pioneers, as well. Generations afterward will reap the blessings of these great sacrifices. Just as many today reap the benefits of the sacrifices of our pioneer forefathers—who went through arduous physical and temporal challenges to secure the blessings of the restored gospel, those who go through strenuous spiritual sacrifices today will bless others in a similar way because of what they've gone through. Their names will one day be honored and praised by those who come after them.

As Dallin H. Oaks once stated,

> Many modern Saints do their pioneering on the frontiers of their own attitudes and emotions. . .Burdens carried in the heart can be just as heavy as those pulled in a handcart. And just as some early pioneers struggled for the benefit of others, so some modern pioneers carry burdens imposed by the transgressions or thoughtlessness of others.

He then describes a letter that came from a woman who had divorced because of her husband's transgression. He stated that, although the ten years following her divorce were a "time of trial, heartache, struggle and loneliness," she described them as a "blessing." He said that she expressed gratitude for her trials and for the things she learned from them. She said:

> It has brought me so close to my Heavenly Father and particularly to the Lord Jesus Christ. It is a feeling that I'm not sure can be expressed in words. I literally came before the Lord with a broken heart and a contrite spirit. No physical pain I have ever experienced has been as painful as the emotional pain I have felt. But each time I feel it, it draws me so close to the Lord because I think of all He suffered, and it makes me so grateful. I love Him with all my heart and soul for His sacrifice and for all He represents.

Many modern spiritual pioneers express similar sentiments, thanking the Lord and Savior, Jesus Christ, for what He has done for them. They can stand as "witnesses" for Him that He truly does "visit" His people "in their afflictions" so that they can "bear up their burdens with ease." (Mosiah 24:14-15)

10

"He Did Heal Them Every One"
(3rd Nephi 17:9)

Dear (Wife):

When our son was just a little boy of four or five years old we were on the driveway with an old skateboard. He was sitting on the skateboard and I was pushing him for a ride. There was a gentle slope to the long driveway so I pointed him down and let him glide down the driveway. I walked behind him for a moment and then determined that I could let him go on his own. However, he trusted that I was behind him the whole time. He was going down the driveway faster and faster and started to realize that I wasn't slowing him down. He was clearly growing uneasy but in his moment of panic he didn't think to put his feet down to stop himself because he was still thinking I would stop him just in time. His skateboard got closer and closer to the edge of the driveway at a faster and faster speed. By the time I realized he didn't know I wasn't behind him, I was out of reach to help him. He hit the end of the driveway at a speed that pushed him off the skateboard and thumped his head on the hard curbside. I ran down and tried to comfort him. He started to cry because of the bump on his head. He had trusted that I would stop him. When he looked at me he was confused and his pure, innocent eyes said, "Why did you hurt me?"

The biggest challenge of my life has been to see your beautiful innocent face and try to answer that same question, "Why did you hurt me?"

I am guilty of adultery.

I know what you're thinking. Of course infidelity is a far more serious injury than a bump on the head. It is especially painful when you didn't see it coming and you trusted that I would be there for you. My analogy is more to illustrate in a small way the awful pain I feel for having betrayed the innocent. I wish I had a better answer than what I will share. Nevertheless, here is my response. I hope and pray you will forgive me.

"Why did you hurt me?"

I now know how participation in pornography can hurt you. It is a breech of our marital vows, of course. But it also gives you the uneasy feeling that you might not measure up—a rejection of your physical offering. I have learned how being physically attractive means so much to a woman and is part of her identity—much more so than a man. I have also learned that the deception can be just as devastating as the participation itself. When you share everything with someone, when you take vows with someone, you literally become "as one." To realize that the person you trusted implicitly has then torn that partnership in two becomes as painful as if you really had physically torn a heart into pieces. That separation is devastating to a woman because a woman risks much more than a man emotionally, physically, financially, and in most every other way.

With the amputation of a marital covenant, there is also the spiritual infection that precedes and follows the sin. I became less interested in spiritual things. I was sloppy in my church assignments. I looked for reasons not to go. I became self-centered and criticized you for not catering to my convenience. I belittled your attempts to be spiritual and I found reasons to spend time *away from home and the chaos of raising kids. When you raised your concerns, I brushed them off as nagging. And for awhile you might have even questioned yourself based on my criticism. You tried harder only to see me slip away even more. I criticized you, the church, your extended family, and the people I worked with. I became so wrapped up in self that there wasn't much room for anyone else. I am sorry. I hope you can forgive me.*

"Why did you hurt me?"

Because I did something that I know in my heart is wrong, I looked for rationale. I had to rationalize my actions and in that rationalization I may have blamed you. I know that isn't right. As part of my repentance process, I have come to realize that I can't blame others for my own decisions. I am sorry. I hope you can forgive me.

I also deceived you. I rationalized that it was a private thing; therefore, my repentance would stay private. I knew what I was doing would hurt you, therefore, "What you didn't know wouldn't hurt you." I determined to put pornography out of my life, fix it so you would never know the difference and spare you the anguish. That was also how I justified not confessing everything to the bishop. If he knew then our whole family's world would cave in. You and the kids would be hurt and branded social outcasts. I rationalized that it was my duty to buffer you from that reality.

But keeping that secret was the very device Satan needed to keep me from "fixing it." Secrecy is a big part of the allure, obsession and addiction of pornography. Secrecy is what allowed the very poison that I was rationalizing I was trying to protect you from. Confession to the bishop was the best thing I could have done. Confession to you was so counter-intuitive for me, since my repentance was undertaken to protect and preserve you and our family. But I have come to see that confession to you and eliminating dishonesty was also important to break the spell of pornography. It also opened my eyes to the real consequences of my sin. I am sorry. I hope you can forgive me.

I rationalized that although pornography is a sin, it isn't THE sin. I drew these crazy lines and then rationalized that as long as I didn't cross that particular line, I was okay. But the line kept getting further and further out. As I darkened in sin, the lines got fuzzier. What I wouldn't have considered at one point became the safe zone at a deeper point. The Lord's line is clear, "If you have lusted after a woman in your heart, you have committed adultery." I am sorry. I hope you can forgive me.

My decisions and choices were not because you weren't pretty enough or sexy enough. It wasn't because you didn't listen to me or treat me right. It wasn't because you weren't fulfilling my emotional needs. It wasn't about you or anything you should have said or done. You didn't "make me do it." It was nothing personal. And that is the point. Pornography makes one impersonal. It detaches its victims from their own feelings and hooks them to pretend relationships that are not relationships at all. It isn't about you. My decisions were not a result of any problems we might have had in our marriage. They contributed to the problems and compounded them. I am sorry. I hope you can forgive me.

"Why did you hurt me?"

I didn't mean to hurt you. I thought pornography was only hurting me. I was too detached, self-absorbed, and "impersonal" to see that within a sacred partnership, hurting myself was hurting you. I am sorry. I hope you can forgive me.

I can't take the hurt away. I have learned that I can't fix it. But I know the Savior can. I love you. I will never hurt you again in this way. I will do everything I can to make it up to you. But only the Savior can help you love again. I am so sorry. I hope you can forgive me.

Your Husband

As illustrated by the foregoing true letter of a husband to his wife, there are many situations where couples are grappling with the deep devastation of sexual sin but are trying desperately to rebuild marriages and relationships through the grace and mercy of our Savior. Though it is a painful, complicated process that has resulted in countless casualties along the way, the Lord in His infinite wisdom has taken many of these broken, lifeless relationships and resurrected them to a fullness and completeness both parties have never experienced before. It has happened to many—and is currently happening to many—who have turned to the Lord through the process of healing.

One woman said of her renewed marital relationship, "My husband is a perfect example of someone who has been healed. I feel like I have been married to two different men—the one at the first of our marriage and the one I'm married to right now. There's no comparison. My husband is so different than what he was before. He's kind, considerate, caring, humble—he's amazing. He's shown me that it can be done (the overcoming of sexual sin)."

There are many transgressors who testify of the Savior's saving power that has freed them from the oppressive bondage of sin and iniquity. Many spouses who have had shattered hearts have spoken of the wholeness and healing that have come to them from the Savior, as well. The healing the Savior offers to those who have been left alone after sexual sin is just as real, deep and lasting.

One woman spoke of the time when "I felt like I would never be happy again. The anguish in my heart (from her husband's betrayal) seemed impossible to overcome. I could never foresee the day where what had happened wouldn't affect me. I thought I'd never find joy in this life again—or get enjoyment out of anything I did. One day as I was carrying some of my deepest anguish, the Lord opened up in my mind a vision of the time when I would feel whole and free of the sorrow—when I would be independent of the hurt that seemed to entrap me. I clung to this image through continuing days of heartache and devastation."

She concludes, "Where I'm at today seems impossible to believe when I remember how I used to feel. I'm not crippled by the pain of the past anymore. I'm independent of my husband and his oppression of me. I find joy and enjoyment in life again—sometimes more than I did before—especially through my children. I'm so grateful that the Lord let me see, in the midst of my pain, that this would happen to me and that there would be healing and wholeness. The Lord doesn't lie when He says He can bring this about. I have felt it in my own life."

As one marriage counselor said, "I have seen miracles happen in relationships (scarred by sexual sin) through the atonement." Another man said, after his wife's betrayal and their subsequent attempts to heal, "I feel like Jacob in the *Old Testament*. He waited fourteen years for his wife. I feel I've waited fourteen years for the wife I've wanted, and I feel I have her today."

This type of healing with the Savior's help can be illustrated symbolically in a dream the Prophet Joseph Smith once had. Wilford Woodruff summarized this dream, entitling it, "The Prophet's Dream—Troubled Waters Overcome." The prophet described an incident in which he went out in "raging waves" that he said he believed he could stay afloat in, despite others claiming he would drown. He said:

> I had swam but a short distance when a towering wave overwhelmed me for a time; but I soon found myself on the top of it, and soon I met the second wave in the same way; and for a while I struggled hard to live in the midst of the storm and waves, and soon found I gained upon every wave, and skimmed the torrent better; and I soon had power to swim with my head out of the water: so the waves did not break over me at all, and I found that I had swam a great distance. . . .I was soon enabled to swim with my head and shoulders out of the water, and I could swim as fast as any steamboat. (*History of the Church,* pp. 194-195)

So it can be with others who have had to deal with the "raging waves" that come from sexual sin. They can learn, through our Savior, to learn to "swim" with their "head(s) out of the water. . .a great distance" where "the waves will not break over [them] at all." (Ibid.) Although the initial progress may seem daunting and ultimate healing impossible, once one begins to move forward in a direction with the Savior, there is great acceleration and progress.

A personal allegory of one woman further illustrates the healing that can come after there have been deep trials or adversities that have come from sexual sin. She said:

> No matter what befalls us in this mortal existence, I know that if we tap into our Father's strength and His saving plan for each of us, we cannot be destroyed. One day I was taking a walk with my young daughter and I saw a woman standing on her lawn, kicking at something beneath her foot and frowning deeply. It looked so strange to see the woman standing there like that, so I asked her, "Is everything okay?"
>
> She threw up her arms and said, "I had this tree growing in my front yard. The roots were getting everywhere so I cut it down below its base, hoping it would die. I even got a full bottle of poison and ran it through the root system, but it didn't even phase it. I don't know what to do to get rid of it. It just won't die."
>
> When I walked away, the analogy of this tree struck me. There may have been hard and bad things that happened to that tree; it was cut down, poisoned and hurt in every way imaginable, but its roots still grew strong and deep. It couldn't be destroyed. So it can be with us. In our lives, many times we might feel we have been "cut down below the base" and even sometimes "poisoned" by events that have happened in our lives because of the terrible choices of others. But if our roots grow deep in our Father in Heaven and we trust that He loves us and has our lives planned out and that we are in His hands, we can become strong and unbreakable—through Him.
>
> I feel this happened to me after my husband's infidelity. What occurred literally seemed to poison my soul and felt like it would destroy me. But as I sank my roots deep in my Father and Savior, I found strength to keep holding on. The thing I feared most happened to me

but it didn't destroy me. Instead, I feel I've discovered the foundation that will never fall. I've become whole once more through my Father and my Savior.

Not only can victims come to taste the healing power of the Lord's atonement, transgressors can, as well. Spencer W. Kimball, in the *Miracle of Forgiveness,* stated, "Sometimes. . .when a repentant one looks back and sees the ugliness, the loathsomeness of the transgression, he is almost overwhelmed and wonders, 'Can the Lord ever forgive me? Can I ever forgive myself?' But when one reaches the depths of despondency and feels the hopelessness of his position, and when he cries out to God for mercy in helplessness but in faith, there comes a still, small, but penetrating voice whispering to his soul, 'Thy sins are forgiven thee.'" (p. 344)

As Isaiah has stated, "Though your sins be as scarlet, they shall be as white as snow." (Isaiah 1:18) This is an enduring promise the Lord has given to His lost sons and daughters who are striving to find Him once more. They can trust in His eternal joy in those who become "established again in the way of his righteousness." (Alma 7:4)

The Freedom That Comes From Forgiveness

Countless sons and daughters of God can testify of the spiritual freedom and divine healing that comes from forgiving others who have deeply wronged them because of sexual sin. Though this "forgiveness" does not mean living with the injustice of continuing sin or putting up with mistreatment, it does free those offended from carrying the burdens of judgment, retribution or revenge, allowing them to turn transgressors and their choices over to the Savior.

One woman spoke of the experience she had as she glimpsed forgiveness as a necessary freeing gift she needed to give herself. She said, "During the time I was struggling with forgiving (a certain person because of an affair), I attended a class in which the instructor gave the parable of the unforgiving debtor. This parable hit me profoundly because the instructor put it into terms I could understand. He spoke of how a certain man owed the king ten thousand talents. With one talent equaling seventy-five pounds, if we applied that to the gold rate of today, the sum that came from that debt would equal millions of dollars. In other words, this man could have started paying everything he made on the day he began working and would have never come close to repaying the debt he owed.

"The man pleaded for mercy because of this impossible debt and the king forgave him. But then that same man went to his servant who owed him one hundred pence. At that time, one pence equaled about one day's wage—so perhaps his servant owed him one hundred days' wage. When his servant came to this man and asked for forgiveness and patience in paying his debt, the man wouldn't offer the same mercy the king had offered. He cast him into prison. Debtor's prison, at that time, was essentially a death sentence. So here this man who had been forgiven millions of dollars in debt essentially turned around and would not forgive hundreds of dollars of debt that had been owed to him."

She continues, "That day, listening to the story, I suddenly realized in my heart that forgiveness needed to be a necessary change in me—for me and my salvation and wholeness. It wasn't just for (the transgressor) that I was struggling to forgive. Christ literally paid debts we cannot pay—amounting to millions of dollars. The few debts we are owed by others need to be forgiven for our own sake and for our own good and freedom. I felt deep within my heart forgiveness was needed just as much for me as (this transgressor)." This woman had learned, as the scriptures say, to "let God judge between me and thee, and reward thee according to thy deeds" (D&C 64:11) instead of taking judgment into her own hands and carrying the burden of not forgiving.

One woman described the freedom that comes from forgiveness in a poem she wrote after her husband's unfaithfulness to her. She said:

> Forgiveness is a special gift
> I want to give to you

But the pain and hurt you've caused
Make me feel unable to.

It may take awhile to trust you,
To show you that I care.
My heart is broken and tender,
My soul feels empty, bare.

But I love the Lord completely
He knows my every thought.
He sees my heart's confusion
With his blood our sins were bought.

To reach out, to forgive you
I must reach out to Him in belief
That He'll strengthen and comfort and listen
In Him I'll find relief.

The Lord has shown me your struggles,
Your desire to be clean once more.
The Spirit of true forgiveness
Is beginning to open my door.

Forgiveness truly is, as Neal A. Maxwell once stated, "Refusing to hold hostage those whom the Lord seeks to set free!" (*Ensign,* Nov. '91, p. 32) It is freeing and emancipating, not binding and hurtful—although the process of getting to that point will be burdensome and challenging. Yet, as Lucy Mack Smith, the mother of the prophet Joseph Smith, once said, "Salvation is worth as much now as it was in the beginning of the work. . . .I find that 'all (would) like (to) purchase (it), (but) few the price will pay.'" (*The Revised and Enhanced History of Joseph Smith,* Proctor, pp. xvii-xviii.) Though learning to forgive can be a long, arduous, excruciating process, it is truly the price to pay for salvation and is worth the unshackled freedom it brings to those who have been hurt by the terrible choices of others.

"I Can 'Forget,' Too"

One woman described an experience in which she learned that one day she would be able to completely forget the pain, horrible emotions and devastation that had occurred because of her husband's deep and prolonged sexual sins. She said:

I had day after day of turmoil (after finding out about her husband). What my husband had done and his choices seemed to be continually before my face. They literally haunted me day and night. As I dealt with this agony, just wishing I could escape my intense pain, I was one day reminded of the scripture that said, "Behold, he who has repented of his sins, the same is forgiven, and I, the Lord, remember them no more." (D&C 58:42, emphasis added) *I began questioning the Lord, "Heavenly Father, if you truly can forget sins that have happened, does that mean that I can forget, too? Does that mean I'll be able to forget all this pain my husband has caused me and all the things he did wrong—those images that now plague me? Will I have a day where I am no longer burdened by this?"*

Suddenly there came into my mind an experience I'd had with a college roommate many years earlier. This roommate and I had become extremely close during our time together, and one day she shared with me the fact she had engaged in some serious moral transgressions. While away at college, she had gone in to the bishop of the student ward and confessed all of her sins to him. The following year when she returned to attend the same university, that same bishop came up to her and said, "I just wanted to tell you something special that has happened to me. I know for certain that last year you came in to me and confessed some problems. I know that you and I spoke. But I want you to know that everything you told me has been taken from my memory. I no longer remember anything you said. I think this experience has been given to me as a testimony of the Lord's forgiveness of you."

As I recalled this story of my roommate, it seemed that the Lord was trying to tell me that "yes"—one day I would forget these terrible things that had happened to me and not remember them. One day the past would not haunt me as it did.

I truly believe this can happen. If the Lord perfectly remembers everything of the past, present and future and yet He remembers sin "no more," then He can help me remember sin no more, too. I've found great peace and comfort in this—that this kind of healing will come to me. I'm waiting and praying for that day.

As another woman stated, "Some miracles of our Savior occur quickly and immediately, but some—probably most—occur over a great deal of time. But the miracles that occur over time are still miracles nonetheless. The way I am to today—the strength I feel, the healing that has come into my heart, my ability to not be hindered by what my husband did—that is a miracle to me."

Many can speak of the miracles that have come through the Savior's atonement in lives once shattered by sexual sin. Although progress may seem slow, we can look at that progress as Ezra Taft Benson once suggested. He said:

> We must be careful, as we seek to become more and more godlike, that we do not become discouraged and lose hope. Becoming Christlike is a lifetime pursuit and very often involves growth and change that is slow, almost imperceptible. The scriptures record remarkable accounts of men whose lives changed dramatically, in an instant, as it were:. . .Paul on the road to Damascus, Enos praying far into the night, King Lamoni. Such astonishing examples of the power to change even those steeped in sin give confidence that the Atonement can reach even those deepest in despair.
>
> But we must be cautious as we discuss these remarkable examples. Though they are real and powerful, for every Enos, and for every King Lamoni, there are hundreds and thousands of people who find the process of repentance much more subtle, much more imperceptible. Day by day they move closer to the Lord, little realizing they are building a godlike life. We must not lose hope. (Ensign, Oct. 1989, p. 5)

Hope for the Weary and Downtrodden

Truman G. Madsen in his book, *Five Classics,* gave some statements that can offer great hope and light to those struggling through the burdensome aftermath of sexual sin. He stated:

> On one occasion Brigham Young was approached by two women who were asking for a divorce, and he gave an idealistic response. He said to them: "If that dissatisfied wife would behold the transcendent beauty of person, the Godlike qualities of the resurrected husband she now despises, her love for him would be unbounded and unutterable. Instead of despising him, she would feel like worshipping him. He is so holy, so pure, so perfect, so filled with God in his resurrected body. There will be no dissatisfaction of this kind in the resurrection of the just. The faithful elders will have then proved themselves worthy of their wives, and are prepared then to be crowned gods, to be filled with all the attributes of the gods that dwell in eternity. Could the dissatisfied ones see a vision of the future glorified state of their husbands, love for them would immediately spring up within you, and no circumstance could prevail upon you to forsake them." (Church Historical Document Ms/D/12234)

Truman G. Madsen continues:

> Now, it also works the other way around, that if the husband could only see his wife in her glorified condition, he would be so moved he would feel to worship....Elder James E. Talmage wrote: "...When the frailties and imperfections of mortality are left behind, in the glorified state of the blessed hereafter, husband and wife will administer in their respective stations, seeing and understanding alike"—oh, hasten the day!— "and cooperating to the full in the government of their family kingdom. Then shall woman be recompensed in rich measure for all the injustice that womanhood has

endured in mortality. Then shall woman reign by Divine right, a queen in the resplendent realm of her glorified state, even as exalted man shall stand, priest and king unto the Most High God." And then he adds in full confirmation of what Brother Brigham said: "Mortal eye cannot see nor mind comprehend the beauty, glory, and majesty of a righteous woman made perfect in the celestial kingdom of God" (*Young Woman's Journal, Oct. 1914, 602-3*) (pp. 350-352)

These promises apply to all who have been affected by sexual sin—transgressors, their spouses and families—and also those left alone after the devastation of betrayal who will not miss out on any promised eternal blessings. Truly the Savior can offer the beloved, sacred gift of His true and everlasting healing to all of His children. As Alma once stated, "The Son of God suffereth according to the flesh that he might take upon him the sins of his people, that he might blot out their transgressions according to the power of his deliverance; and now behold, this is the testimony which is in me. . . .*The Lamb of God. . .is mighty to save and cleanse from all unrighteousness.*" (Alma 7:13-14, italics added) As one of the verses in a hymn states:

> *Come unto Jesus, ye heavy laden,*
> *Care-worn and fainting, by sin oppressed*
> *He'll safely guide you unto that haven*
> *Where all who trust him may rest.* (117)

All who come to Him truly can rest in His peace, love and gentle care. Therefore, as the Savior promises, "Gird up your loins and be faithful, and ye shall overcome all things, and be lifted up at the last day." (D&C 78:22) "Behold, I, the Lord, declare unto you, and my words are sure and shall not fail, that they shall obtain it." (D&C 64:31)

All who do come to our Savior may obtain the promise of His everlasting grace and mercy. Those who have experienced this will come to glory in our Savior's and Father's sacred names and will, with the "holy angels, and them who are sanctified before his throne" worship "God, and the Lamb. . .forever and ever" (D&C 76:21) for the saving work they have done among the children of men.